THIS DEATH BY D.

William Kloefkorn

This Death by Drowning

University of Nebraska Press : Lincoln and London

Chapter 3 originally appeared as "A Gathering of
Rains" in *Prairie Schooner* 69, no. 2 (summer 1995):
40–56, © 1995 by the University of Nebraska Press.
© 1997 by the University of Nebraska Press. All rights
reserved. Manufactured in the United States of
America. ⊗ First Nebraska paperback printing: 2001

The Library of Congress has cataloged the
hardcover edition as follows:
Kloefkorn, William
This death by drowning / William Kloefkorn.
p. cm. ISBN 0-8032-2736-1 (cl. : alk. paper)   1. Title.
PS3561.L626T48   1997   813'.54–dc21   96-53543 CIP
ISBN 0-8032-7799-7 (pa: alk. paper)

I am haunted by waters.—Norman Maclean, *A River Runs Through It*

One week before I entered Miss Katie Puls's first-grade room to begin an education that I pray never ends, I fell into Harold Simpson's cow-pasture pond and came within one gulp of drowning.

My father saved me. He was fishing at another pond about a hundred yards away when I tumbled in, and my mother's frantic soprano brought him running. He was wearing blue overalls and a blue long-sleeved workshirt and brown ankle-high workboots and was still clutching his rod and reel when he jumped in. The water not far below the surface was cool because the pond was spring fed. I was going down for the third time when I felt my father's hand like a two-pronged grappling hook under my chin. The next thing I knew, I was lying face down in the pasture, water gushing from my mouth as if from a cistern.

Hearsay and fabrication: what I don't remember I attribute to someone else, and when that fails I fabricate. Father's hand under my chin felt like a two-pronged grappling hook because two of his fingers, his middle ones, were missing. They had been twisted off in an accident that somehow involved a pulley and a chain and a half-filled bucket of 10-weight motor oil. Father worked for Harper County in the state of Kansas, circa 1936, and the accident occurred in mid-August. Mother learned about it from my father's foreman, Ira Wyrick, who stood on the side porch of our modest home talking behind a screen door held together with string and strips of white adhesive tape.

"He's in the hospital in Anthony," Mr. Wyrick said. "He's going to be all right. He's under the care of Dr. Galloway."

I was four. I stood beside my mother, trying my best to take everything in. My mother was, and is, a substantial German woman who is long-haul strong and short-term weak. She had been in the kitchen stirring something on the stove when Mr. Wyrick knocked on the screen door. She went to the door wiping her hands on her apron. I went with her. I was so close beside her that to the naked eye there must have been no visible seam. She smelled like butter and milk and onion.

"Here's Ralph's lunch bucket," Mr. Wyrick said. "We saved the fingers. They fell into a bucket of motor oil. They're wrapped in a napkin."

When he left, my mother for a short while went all to pieces. She sat on a kitchen chair, the lunch bucket on a table before her, sobbing into the apron. She had been stirring potato soup, small pieces of potato in whole milk laced with bacon and butter and bits of onion, and perhaps the aroma in her apron, as she raised it to dry her eyes, augmented the tears. A rooster decorated a corner of the apron, a rooster put there with bright red yarn manipulated by the fingers of my mother's mother, Anna.

Mother wept passionately into the apron. She wept, and she spoke to God. "God, why did this happen? God, what are we going to do?"

Mother believed in God, though she herself did not go to church. She had gone to church as a child and as an adolescent, but when she married my father and gave birth to my sister, then to me, and finally my brother, she passed on that responsibility to her children. But in moments of crisis she remembered bits and pieces of her catechism, often using them to her own advantage.

Case in point: the burning of the outhouse.

I had not intended to burn down our outhouse. I liked it. It was an ancient structure made of pine, a two-holer, and it leaned just slightly to the south. To my knowledge it had never been painted. In the summer it was a pleasant and private place in which to indulge one's deepest meditations and memorize selected portions of the Sears catalog. Such a place deserved a more noble demise than death by fire.

I had stood behind it one hot afternoon in early July, lighting Black Cat firecrackers and tossing them with practiced nonchalance into the atmosphere. Beside me, abutting the outhouse, was a crosshatched pile of discarded lumber and a couple of cardboard boxes and at least one thistle, a stray that found its way across Shorty Cleveland's back yard and somehow through the barbed-wire fence to come to rest in our boardpile. Perhaps, having exploded a Black Cat, I inadvertently dropped a live match on the thistle, and perhaps that ignited thistle somehow ignited a slat that perhaps put to flame an extremely dry one-by-four that perhaps—and so on. In any case, the outhouse suddenly blossomed into a two-holer inferno, and almost literally in the twinkling of an eye my place of privacy and of meditation had been reduced to ashes.

What stunned me was my mother's reaction. She neither rebuked nor flayed me. Instead, she placed the blame where probably it belonged—on Divine Providence.

3

"God," she said, looking at my father, whose eyes were every bit as green as mine, "wants us to have an indoor facility."

To this day I do not understand fully how our indoor facility came finally to be. I attribute a part of it to my father's swearing—loud and frequent and utterly confident of impunity. Another part I attribute to stubbornness, to my father's absolute refusal to quit, no matter the odds against him. And a final part—to complete this triumvirate—I attribute to our neighbor, Merlin Ogden, who actually owned a pipe wrench and a shovel and a toolbox with honest-to-goodness tools inside it, and who apparently, when it came to plumbing, knew a hawk from a handsaw.

So day by day, week by week, an hour here and an hour there, our bathroom evolved until at last it came to full fruition. And my father looked upon it, and was pleased. Perhaps inordinately so. And I looked into his green eyes and I thought, If this is what swearing can lead to, then I must learn to swear.

Much later I wrote of this epiphany, ending the poem like this:

Its porcelain bowl
So beautiful
It might have been Christ feeding the multitude.

A fourth part must be added to the triumvirate: my mother's initial insistence that the burning of our outhouse had been a signal from the Almighty: Go ye therefore and provide thyself, and thyself's husband and thy husband's and thyself's children, a decent indoor facility for thy collective privacy and meditations. Not to mention comfort.

Such a woman cannot reasonably be expected to weep indefinitely into an apron. So before long my mother collected herself, piece by piece, and when she was whole again she called me to her to tell me what Ira Wyrick had told both of us:

"Your father is in the hospital in Anthony. He's going to be all right. He's under the care of Dr. Galloway."

She arose and went to the stove, where she stood for a long time stirring the potato soup, which had begun to boil.

Father kept the fingers. He placed them in a mason jar filled with formaldehyde and displayed them on a shelf behind the Warm-Morning coalburner. One evening he gave me my first lecture on the workplace anatomy of mortality.

"Look at those fingers," he said, and I did. "Work for the county long enough," he said, "and you'll end up strung out in bottles all the way from hell to breakfast."

I remember wondering, What does that mean, *all the way from hell to breakfast?* I tried to imagine my body parts in jars of formaldehyde strung out *all the way from hell to breakfast,* but I had trouble forming a clear and coherent image of hell. So I settled for a shelf that extended from behind the Warm-Morning to the east wall of the kitchen.

Touchstones. Matthew Arnold writes of literary touchstones—those most distinctive lines from those most distinctive masters, lines in the high style against which all other lines might best be judged. He quotes lines from Shakespeare and Milton and others as examples. From Shakespeare's *Henry IV:*

Wilt thou upon the high and giddy mast
Seal up the ship-boy's eyes, and rock his brains
In cradle of the rude imperious surge. . . .

Again from Shakespeare—Hamlet's dying request to Horatio:

If thou didst ever hold me in thy heart,
Absent thee from felicity awhile,
And in this harsh world draw thy breath in pain
To tell my story. . . .

From Milton's *Paradise Lost:*

Darken'd so, yet shone
Above them all the archangel; but his face
Deep scars of thunder had intrench'd, and care
Sat on his faded cheek. . . .

I would like to add to Arnold's concept of the literary touchstone a touchstone of my own—the experience that leaves an imprint on one or more of the senses so indelible that it significantly influences a large portion of what the individual thinks and does and writes for the rest of his lovely and tormented life. It is the epiphany that will not go away. It is the cold water in the pond in Simpson's pasture as I was about to go under for the third time: at that moment I learned forever the potential significance of *wet,* learned forever the intricacies of water—its glories, its jests, its riddles. Water is now the tactile touchstone by which I measure all degrees of submersion, and I respect this touchstone as Arnold respected a glorious handful of lines from the masters.

Confession: probably my father had not been fishing with a rod and reel; more likely he had been using a cane pole. On the way to the ponds that day in August I heard him say that, next to nightcrawlers, grasshoppers are best for catfishing. So

6

I spent my time chasing bait, Mother having cast out a line with a red bobber attached, Father having chosen the pond about a hundred yards to the north.

The ultimate challenge presented itself when a grasshopper the size of a Hereford whizzed up and away from my feet, described a high arc, and landed, I thought, at the edge of the pond.

I went to my knees, then to my belly; I began to execute what sixteen years later, as a private in boot camp at Quantico, I learned as *snooping and pooping.* When I reached that spot on the edge of the pond where I thought the prize grasshopper had landed, I paused and raised my head and surveyed the terrain. No grasshopper. So I moved slightly beyond the edge and looked down. There, only inches from the water, rested the hopper.

I took a deep breath, then lunged at the grasshopper as if taking him prisoner were a matter of life and death.

Much later, after my mother had regained her composure and become genuinely convinced that her older son was not dead by reason of water, I heard her describe my descent: "He went flying," she said, "ass over appetite into the water."

Even today I try to see myself flying *ass over appetite,* but the image blurs. *Appetite?* What does that mean, to go flying *ass over appetite?*

When I hit the water I floundered in what I thought to be the direction of the shore. But I was disoriented. So instead of floundering shoreward I floundered in the direction of deeper water, and soon in fear and confusion I became dead weight, going under, down and under, learning the hard way the touchstone of wetness, of baptism by total submersion, until a lifeline with two fingers missing found me and snagged my chin and bore me upward into the sweet ambience of oxygen, onto a pasture of bunchgrass beneath a blue sky vast and cloudless and into a life that having begun and ended began again.

Add these lines to Arnold's listing, being careful to acknowledge Stevie Smith:

I was much too far out all my life
And not waving but drowning.

If there is magic on this planet, it is contained
in water. — Loren Eiseley, *The Immense Journey*

Then my brother John takes his turn. We are nine and eleven.
In precisely one year President Truman will say yes, and the
universe will never be the same: ATOMIC BOMB DROPPED ON
HIROSHIMA. I will deliver this headline to sixty-seven subscribers to the *Wichita Beacon,* my bundle of *Beacon*s having
been dropped off at the Champlin station by Mr. Evans, a tall
friendly Norwegian who through all of the war's demands
for rationing always managed somehow to equip his Dodge
with whitewall tires.

Even before my brother took his turn at drowning, events
had conspired to remind me that the magic contained in
water can be blacker than black. It had been five years since
I floundered and gasped in the cool spring-fed water of
Harold Simpson's cow-pasture pond — but what is time, after
all, to those immortals who have nothing better to do than to
spin and measure and cut the threads of mortal lifelines?
Oedipus ruled Thebes, and ruled it well, for more than
twenty years before the gods saw fit to put another kink in his
royal lifeline; to the gods, time is indeed the stream one goes
a-fishing in, as Thoreau more or less phrased it. So the five-
year interim between my rescue from Simpson's Pond and
the outbreak of the Second World War must have been less

9

than a ripple on the surface of the water the gods wet their immortal worms in.

For me, the war began on Monday, 8 December, a few minutes after ten hundred hours. I was in Grade 4, under the tutelage of Miss Faye Vermilia. Miss Vermilia was not young. She was thin and perhaps tall. According to the older boys in the bathroom, she wore a wig. She was soft spoken, her voice never rising beyond a whisper. But she was the most effective disciplinarian ever assembled by egg and sperm. I really don't know why she was so effective, but she was. Maybe it was her eyes. Or the way her voice inflected. Or the angle at which she held her ruler, an instrument not unlike the swagger stick that DI sonofabitch at Quantico, Virginia, circa 1954, wielded against my knees when I was out of step.

In any case, when Miss Vermilia spoke, the world listened. And my world at that time was a niche in south-central Kansas, population more or less seven hundred, half a dozen churches, and a town ordinance extremely unfavorable to anything not white or Protestant.

At oh nine hundred we were to be seated at our desks, our hands atop the desks with palms joined as if at prayer, our eyes focused straight ahead, our mouths shut. When Miss Vermilia called the roll, whispered it, we were to respond with nothing saucier than "Here!"

I was sitting at my desk with my hands at prayer when Miss Vermilia began the roll call. My eyes were focused straight ahead, though only moments earlier they had wandered to the left just far enough to notice that the class deviant, Jackie Dellman, was absent. This puzzled me. I was certain that I had seen Jackie when I arrived at school around oh eight fifty. He was on the playground, his hands in his pockets, watching the merry-go-round as if it were an oddity that defied human understanding. I hadn't thought much about it, because Jackie was a loner, a free spirit that viewed independence as a more precious commodity than, say, homework or class standing. And so it was that Jackie was repeating Grade 4 under the tutelage of Miss Faye Vermilia.

So I was surprised to have noted that Jackie Dellman was not in his seat. Though in most respects a nonconformist and a tough (he loved to pick fights with upperclassmen, then beat their socks off), Jackie nonetheless, like the rest of us, respected whatever it was in Miss Vermilia that commanded respect.

Now, as Miss Vermilia calls the roll, you must see the room in which the roll call is taking place. It is a square room on the second floor of the building that housed all levels of my hometown's educational system. Along the north wall is a blackboard clean as a Presbyterian's hands, a blackboard that in several weeks will bear the words of the first poem ever to hit me point blank. The author: William Allingham. The title: "Four Ducks on a Pond." The poem:

Four ducks on a pond,
A grass bank beyond,
A blue sky of spring,
White clouds on the wing;
What a little thing
To remember for years—
To remember with tears!

Miss Vermilia had written the poem meticulously on the westernmost rectangle of the blackboard, and in the upper left corner she had printed in bold white letters, PLEASE SAVE. You looked at those words, PLEASE SAVE, and somehow — call it osmosis, call it intuition — you knew that they had been infused by Miss Vermilia with something more than mere flake of chalk. I personally would not have erased those words for all the tea in China.

And besides, I loved the poem. It made sense. I had never seen four ducks on a pond, as I assume the poet had, but I had seen its equivalent, and the equivalent was registered on my brain like a hieroglyphic in granite.

A blue sky broken only by three limbs jutting from the trunk of a mulberry tree. This image was the first to greet me after I had been pumped free of water and rolled over onto my back, my father above me with his two fingers missing, almost smiling. I had opened my eyes to see, first, the immense blueness beyond the three limbs of the mulberry, and, next, the grappler that had saved me — grappler connected to its owner, almost smiling. Now I measure all blueness against that blueness, all hands against my father's hands, all reticence against that near-smile on my father's lips.

So when one morning shortly before the end of recess I came upon Herschel Skaggs erasing the poem, and tore into him and bloodied his nose and probably would have maimed him further had not Miss Vermilia restrained me, you can maybe understand my reaction sufficiently to forgive if not applaud it. Skaggs was a Neanderthal who, with blood draining from his primal nose, for a short time acted nearly human.

The west wall of the room was comprised of windows overlooking the playground, where I had seen Jackie Dellman watching, as if mesmerized, the merry-go-round. At the back of the room was a line of hangers for our coats. Our desks were combinations of chairs and desktops, with drawers beneath the desks for our pads and pencils and books. There were twenty-three of us in Grade 4, and the desks were arranged in five straight rows, five desks to a row. I sat in the third row, just to the right of Jackie, with Marlene Walters in front of me and John Burgess behind. Donna Grace Davis, a champion speller if there ever was one, sat at my right.

Miss Vermilia in a room filled with silence called the roll slowly, softly, deliberately. "Here!" each student at the sound of the appropriate name intoned. "Here!"

Then something beyond peculiar happened: Miss Vermilia erred. She failed to call Jackie Dellman's name. I could hardly believe it. Miss Vermilia—thin, perhaps tall, rock-bottomed and copper-sheathed—had made a mistake, no doubt the first of her not altogether young life. I wanted to correct her, and I believe I did indeed raise my right hand to half-mast before reconsidering.

She finished the roll call and set us to work at my weakest subject, arithmetic. Long division. I was struggling on my first problem when I thought I heard a sound like sniffling. I looked up. At her desk Miss Vermilia sat reading a book whose title I could not decipher.

I returned to the problem. Then, again, the sniffling. I looked up. Miss Vermilia was deep into her reading. I looked to my right. Donna Grace, Queen of Spellers, appeared to be going through the problems as easily as if she had been confronted with *occurrence.* In front of me Marlene Walters's long curly hair was bobbing in a sea of effort. At my left Jackie Dellman's desk was empty.

I returned to the problem. The more I worked at it, the longer its division seemed to grow. Then, again, the sniffling.

The distracting sound was coming from the back of the room. I took a chance: I turned my head as if a periscope, first ninety degrees to the right, then the same number of degrees to the left. The second turning revealed the distraction—Jackie Dellman, standing in the southwest corner of the room, his hands in his pockets, his nose running, his moist eyes looking out the window fixedly, as if the entire world were an oddity that defied human understanding.

Now the long division became suddenly impossibly longer. Before me, on the desk, lay a dividend half the length of my arm, waiting for a quotient; behind me stood my tough square-jawed colleague, sniffling; and at the head of the room sat Miss Vermilia, doing absolutely nothing to set things straight.

At recess at ten hundred hours one of the quotients emerged—a sheet of Kodak paper in a pan of developer wondrously registering a distinct though troubling picture. Jackie Dellman's older brother, not long before ten hundred hours the day before, had been aboard one of the ships sunk by the Japanese at Pearl Harbor.

Thus did Jackie Dellman receive such special dispensation from Miss Vermilia, who had not erred, after all. Jackie was not certain which ship his brother was aboard; the *Arizona* and the *Oklahoma* were reported sunk, total losses, and a number of other ships had taken heavy casualties. The odds in favor of Jackie's brother did not seem favorable.

Long division. Who or what is the dividend? The divisor? "Who in this bowling alley," as Edward Taylor put it, "bowled the sun?" If I divide Vice-Admiral Nagumo, commander of the Japanese attack force (363 planes in two waves), by Admiral Kimmel, officer in charge of the base at Pearl Harbor (seven battleships moored neatly in a row at the center of the harbor), will the quotient be the deaths of more than 2,400 Americans? I bite first the eraser on my yellow Ticonderoga pencil, next my lower lip. Or this: 104 high-level bombers equipped with torpedoes, plus 135 dive-bombers, 40 torpedo bombers, and 81 fighters, divided by a handful of disbelieving Sunday-morning Yanks, plus three aircraft carriers that weren't there: can the quotient fairly be called an *answer*?

What troubled me most at the time, and what yet haunts me—as did the currents of the Big Blackfoot haunt Norman Maclean—is my own conjectural image of hundreds upon hundreds of sailors drowning deep in the bespoiled water near the island of Oahu, each of them going down that third and final time, none of them with a father sufficient to save them. Baptism by smoke and fire. Baptism by total immersion.

So that is one of the infrequent but enormous epiphanies that reminds me of the comparatively tame but initial one, those moments at Simpson's Pond when I was "not waving but drowning."

Now I must answer a question that I can't resist asking: Why in the name of all that is reasonable hadn't I known about Pearl Harbor before Monday?

Simple addition, I think. First, I had no connection whatsoever with anyone or anything political, anything even roughly related to world affairs, an ignorance that I inherited from my parents—who inherited it from their parents, all of

15

whom had a familiar if not palatable excuse: they were too poor and most of the time too isolated to concern themselves with much of anything beyond their own family gyre. Add to this that they had little formal education. My mother finished high school, but my father never started; an only son, he stayed home to help manage the two-cow farm.

Add one thing more: the most exciting weekend of my life.

Though poor, we nonetheless had two relatives with money enough to drive to Niagara Falls for their honeymoon, then return to the midlands to enjoy a long weekend at the Grande Cabins on the outskirts of Wichita. Even more amazing is that they invited my family, all five of us, to spend Saturday and part of Sunday with them. O sweet Jesus! My parents did not immediately accept the invitation, of course; such a pilgrimage would entail more preparation and more mental toughness than perhaps we were capable of.

But eventually they said yes; eventually we piled our scrubbed and anxious selves into our battered Chevrolet and with a song and a shrug we kissed the village of Attica, in the County of Harper, State of Kansas, goodbye.

Father with his tin ear intact sang swatches of "The Great Speckled Bird," "The Wabash Cannonball," and "I'm Saving up Coupons." He rolled his own Raleigh cigarettes, and he did save the coupons—though I never knew him to mail them. Many nights I lay awake wondering what might happen to us should my father send away his Raleigh coupons. Would we receive a bundle of cash the size of, say, a washtub made in Wheeling, West Virginia? A new Hawthorne bicycle? A Red Ryder BB gun? A couple of new fingers to replace those my father lost to the pulley and the chain and the half-filled bucket

16

of 10-weight motor oil? (And what does that mean, anyway, to be *10-weight*?) "I'm saving up coupons," he would sing—was singing now, as we rattled northeastward in the general direction of the Grande Cabins—"to buy one of those. A coupon redeemer, I'll die, I suppose."

I suppose. But not just now. Just now we are going where I have never gone before, to the outskirts of a bona fide city. To a cabin being rented by my Aunt Vivian and Uncle Elmer, who have money enough to rent it, who are generous enough to share it with their indigent relatives.

I am two-thirds excited, one-third apprehensive. What if we have a flat tire? Not that my father can't fix it; but he takes automobile breakdowns personally. He curses and kicks things and inevitably ends up with grease and oil and grit on his body all the way from hell to breakfast, from ass to appetite. Or what if things don't go well at the cabin? And where are we going to sleep? What do you say to people newly married? And what if . . .

But two-thirds are more than one-third. Simple arithmetic. So what the hell? I give excitement its full rein, and the weekend truly begins.

Henry Vaughan said it like this:

I cannot reach it, and my striving eye
Dazzles at it, as at eternity.

So I'll not attempt to describe fully what cannot be fully described. The weekend was, and is, a lovely blur of significance. My Uncle Elmer, a portly young round-faced farmer, 4-F, with an immense smile, established a tone: he gave me and my brother each a souvenir pocket knife, each knife with one beautiful silver blade and a handle in technicolor depicting the Falls. Aunt Vivian gave my sister a souvenir kewpi doll about which my brother and I did not laugh our britches off until we were safely beyond range of unsympathetic ears — until we had climbed halfway up the linden in front of the cabin, that is, where we whittled and guffawed and with careful fingers felt the blades of our knives with a reverence unmatched by church.

Another thing: the day was unseasonably warm. You inhaled and you thought, spring. Kansas is like that — one moment an orthodox grownup, the next moment an infant with its days and nights akimbo. "Love a place like Kansas," someone whose name escapes me wrote, "and you can be content in a garden of raked sand."

I can appreciate that anonymous writer's cynicism: he didn't spend the weekend of 6–7 December 1941 on the outskirts of Wichita at the Grande Cabins. He probably didn't have a younger brother to laugh and whittle with. The poor soul probably didn't even have the wherewithal to do the whittling — a souvenir knife with a beautiful silver blade and a handle in technicolor depicting the Falls. I forgive him.

No doubt the unseasonable weather was a complement to the wellspring of affection that my uncle and aunt seemed to be indulging. They had just returned from their honeymoon. They held hands. Their eyes met. When they smiled, or laughed, they apparently meant it. Once in a while my uncle for no obvious reason would raise his chubby farmer's hand and pat the bun of brunette that Aunt Vivian inherited from my grandmother. Oh, there was something in the air, all right, something more than air itself, and I could sense at least a portion of it at work in my nearly new overalls.

Because "I cannot reach it, and my striving eye / Dazzles at it," I'll stop here and draw the line and observe the sum.

Parents, for several reasons,
oblivious to politics and to
world affairs,
            plus
a view of the skyline of
Wichita, Kansas
            plus
a new souvenir pocket knife,
            plus
the stirrings of passion
            equal
an understandable excuse for
not learning about
Pearl Harbor until Monday,
December 8, around
ten hundred hours. . . .

Simple addition, I think.

But one sum does not a quotient make: I yet could not begin to understand why an emperor with henchmen bearing names like Yamamoto and Nagumo should want to send thousands of innocent bodies to the bottom of a watery grave ten million million times the size of Simpson's Pond. Why should they perish when I survived? And why, if they *must* perish, must their deaths be by water? Year into year I sit at my desk in Miss Vermilia's classroom, the lead in my yellow Ticonderoga moving feverishly against sheet after pulpy sheet of Big Chief paper. The fact that Jackie Dellman's brother survived does little to assuage the problem, does nothing to soften the slow-motion image of cheekbone and thigh, of breastbone and neck, of backbone and kneebone and elbow and fingerbone adrift forever in the hallways and hulls of an otherwise blue and beautiful harbor.

Until the answer comes full circle to become the question:

> *. . . who in this conflagration*
> *First spoke of fire? And who*
> *Will be the last to shout its heat*
> *Into the cool quotient of emptiness?*

Then another dam broke, another sizable spillage occurred, before my brother John took his own turn at drowning.

I had become a legitimate moviegoer; that is, I had found a way to earn enough money so that I could pay, rather than sneak, into the theater. I didn't actually earn money; I instead earned free passes by mowing Mr. Earl W. Shutt's lawn, seven free passes per mowing. Mr. Shutt, who had purchased the movie house from Frank Biberstein, was quiet and pensive and wise, an inveterate cigar-smoker who trusted me to keep track of the mowings and the free passes. This I did, religiously. I mowed the lawn perhaps oftener than necessary, the snicksnicksnick of dull blades trimming buffalograss before it had any honorable chance to do much growing. Into a small notebook I did my entering and my tallying—simple addition, nothing more. Seven + seven + seven equals.

During the summer I accumulated enough free passes to see me through the winter. At first I was careful to show my employer my notebook and its entries; behind a pane of glass at the ticket window Mr. Shutt would squint through the screen of cigar smoke and nod his head. Later, after I had lost the notebook and had fabricated dates and numbers in another one, I took fewer pains to show Mr. Shutt where I stood. I should have realized that Mr. Shutt didn't really give a damn. I had mowed his lawn all summer, and Earl W. Shutt, his wisdom directly related to his generosity, was willing to let me into the theater every night all fall and winter and early spring. I would otherwise have sneaked in, and he would have been too kind to boot me out. In effect, Mr. Shutt was getting his lawn mowed for nothing. One plus one equals two.

Inside that long dark narrow cozy sanctuary called movie house I fell in love with Betty Grable: ask me even now to sing a verse or two of "Diamond Horseshoe." Inside that sanctuary I learned down deep in my heart the magic contained not only in water but in the lexicon of war. Stuka. Kamikaze. Atoll. Panzer. Iwo. Flying Tiger. Allied. Bangalore. Messerschmidt. Sortie. Rising Sun. (Pure magic, pure music—awful and urgent and sometimes bloated with pride, just as often with fear. "Magic," I'll learn more than a few years later, was the undercover name for the successful decoding of messages sent by the Japanese to their agents around the world.) Inside that sanctuary I worshipped at the combat boots of the Marine who alone with his heavy machine gun went to his reward grinning and rat-tat-tatting into hordes of bucked teeth as the credits appeared and the lights in the theater came up too quickly. Inside that sanctuary, in newsreels grim with sepia, I hit beach after beach, now rolling over, now flat on my belly, in my left hand the pin of another grenade on its way to bursting.

But chiefly inside that sanctuary I was haunted by water.

21

First came the drowning of Druscilla Alston (alias Susan Hayward) in *Reap the Wild Wind*. You remember Druscilla: she was a stowaway in the lower hold of a magnificent sailing ship that, having been treacherously sunk, was being somewhat salvaged by Stephen Tolliver (alias Ray Milland) and Captain Jack Stuart (alias John Wayne), rivals who battled not only each other but also a giant squid that confused both issue and water with its inky juices. One of the heroes at last saves the other by sacrificing himself to the squid.

But for me the denouement of the movie involves neither sacrifice nor squid. It is rather that extended deep-water slow-motion moment when the explorers slowly and lightly, as if moonwalkers, shine their undersea lights on a wooden chest from which, through a wide crack at the lid, floats a scarf and strands of hair—long and numerous and the color of salt-water taffy. And we know that, beyond the visible, these delicate strands, serpentining in slow motion, are attached to the scalp of the incomparably lovely stowaway, Druscilla Alston.

Then came the Sullivans.

George T., 29, gunner's mate second class; Francis H., 26, coxswain; Joseph E., 23, seaman second class; Madison A., 22, seaman second class; Albert L., 20, seaman second class.

They were brothers. I had read of their deaths in the *Wichita Beacon,* in stories that carried most of the pitiful details. All five had enlisted on the same day, 3 January 1942. The following month they requested that they be permitted to serve together, and the request was honored. Not many weeks later they found themselves aboard a cruiser, the *Juneau,* one of the ships active in the Battle of Guadalcanal. Earlier, in September, the cruiser had served as an escort for the carrier *Wasp*, and when that ship was sunk by a Japanese submarine the *Juneau* rescued more than 1,800 survivors.

Life's irony, in or out of war: one day the corpsman, next day the corpse. The *Juneau* was hit by a torpedo on my brother's birthday, 12 November, whereupon listing badly it withdrew from battle. The next day the third of three torpedoes from a Japanese submarine, *I-26*, struck the *Juneau* near the point where she had been damaged the day before. "Her magazines exploded," reported the *Beacon*, and the ship sank in twenty minutes. Ten survived. (Add *magazine* to the abbreviated lexicon above. What precisely is a ship's "magazine"? Once in a while, picking up a copy of *Time* or *Newsweek*, I suddenly hear the *Juneau* exploding, the Sullivan brothers and all of their crewmates except ten going under, so steady their deep-green death-green gurgling.)

What the newspaper could not report the film dramatized, and inside that long dark narrow cozy sanctuary called movie house I watched the waters just off Guadalcanal claim the limbs and the torsos of the Sullivans and their comrades. I saw the movie every night until it left town, as if my initial touchstone of wetness needed reinforcement—as if it could never be reinforced enough.

Consolations: a destroyer, *The Sullivans*, was launched on 4 April 1943. And President Roosevelt wrote a personal letter to Mr. and Mrs. Thomas F. Sullivan of Waterloo, Iowa:

I am sure that we all take pride in the knowledge that they fought side by side. As one of your sons wrote, "We will make a team together that can't be beat." It is this spirit which in the end must triumph.

Magic contained in water can be blacker than a cistern, redder than a rooster, whiter than milk or snow.

It was finally my brother's turn to try his hand at drowning. I had given it my best effort at Simpson's Pond; hundreds upon hundreds of startled seamen had succeeded at Pearl Harbor; Druscilla Alston (alias Susan Hayward) had likewise triumphed, her long hair drifting from a stowaway's tomb in the hold of a vanquished ship; and the Sullivan brothers with their undaunted mates had yielded to an exploding of magazines.

I was eleven. My brother was nine. In eight months President Franklin D. Roosevelt, in Warm Springs, Georgia, there to soak his ailing legs in the curative waters of an infamous spa, would die suddenly, leaving the fate of us all to Harry S. Truman. In less than a month after Roosevelt's death and Truman's ascendency, Germany would surrender to the Allies, and in three months after that the *Enola Gay* would drop a 9,000-pound "Little Boy" on Hiroshima. I would deliver the printed report of that event to sixty-seven subscribers to the *Wichita Beacon,* each subscriber that windless day of 6 August 1945 standing on the front porch with one arm extended and both eyes looking through and beyond me, each like Jackie Dellman four years earlier looking to make sense of an oddity that defied human understanding.

President Truman called the bomb "a black rain of ruin," said, "We have spent two billion dollars on the greatest scientific gamble in history—and won." When he made the announcement of the bomb from aboard the *Augusta,* one of the crewmen reportedly said, "I guess I'll be going home a little sooner." A headline declared, SHAVING LOTION SHORTAGE TO END BEFORE AUTUMN. Code name for the experimental explosion of the bomb in New Mexico on 16 July: *Trinity.* In the name of the Father, and of the Son . . .

Delivering the *Beacon* that day I felt like a messenger beyond any form of recall or chastisement; not even Zeus's offspring, Hermes, with wings at his heels, could have rivaled me that day as a bearer of good though peculiar tidings. Good—because our Johnnies at last would come marching home again. Peculiar—because a lid had been lifted on a chest marked "Think Again," and what had escaped was an animal the likes of which we commoners could not quite conceive, much less (or so I believe we feared, however intuitively) contain.

For a week or more, having taken the bundle of papers from the stout hands of Mr. Evans, I sat folding them on a green-slatted bench in the Champlin station. I felt alternately elated and depressed, sometimes each so strong that neither in turn wanted to yield, and they overlapped. My team had been victorious; yet in victory I delivered statistics sufficient to shiver the staunchest spine. Bomb released from 31,000 feet, detonating 45 seconds later at a height of 660 yards over the center of Hiroshima. For 1/10,000 second a heat of 300,000 degrees centigrade was generated, flattening and disintegrating and melting everything—brick and wood and fabric and flesh—within a 2,000-yard radius of the hypocenter. (Add that word now to the lexicon, and, with it, *mushroom* and *fallout* and *half-life, fireball* and *ground zero.* Add *Nagasaki,* alternate to Kokura, spared on 9 August because of a cloud cover, so that according to the Japanese the combined devastations

25

amounted to 240,000 dead—"many expiring," one story reported, "in lingering agony from burns and radiation aftereffects." Add *radiation*. Add *aftereffects*. Add *Fat Man*.)

Clockwise around the fringes of my small hometown I soon would circle, delivering the *Beacon*, bearing the good news with the bad, wanting something more reassuring than a question as the quotient to my long division. I come to this:

> *The circle we finally finish*
> *is never finished. The burned and*
> *wasted bodies of children, though*
> *gone, are never gone.*

But all of that has yet to happen. At the moment I am with my brother at Ely's Sandpit, and with us is our mentor, an older boy with dark hair and the trace of a mustache, behind which, I swear, I can see a young Clark Gable. His name is Carter Leroy Hays—and, though he is the oldest, he is not the first to hit the water. The first is my daredevil brother, John.

We are naked and looking pitifully white—fishbelly white, as Huck Finn might put it. It is a bright afternoon in August, and two of us, my brother and I, are here against the will of our parents. Carter, on the other hand, is entirely free of anything remotely resembling a heavy conscience. His parents are his grandparents, his original mother and father having delivered him into the older couple's care and then apparently, as if liquid, evaporating. The grandparents are old and sedentary and spiritual; given a choice between bulldozer and faith to move a mountain, both without a moment's hesitation would opt for faith. They love their grandson, who failed the fifth grade twice, and they provide evidence of their love by permitting him to do any damn thing he pleases.

Carter is not stupid. He failed the fifth grade twice because the fifth grade failed him: nothing about it could catch and hold his attention. He was an independent spirit and, it seemed to me, a natural-born teacher because he was a natural-born storyteller. He illustrated his stories with his hands, his long and delicate fingers fluttering or not fluttering at all of the precisely right moments, his green eyes (my father's eyes were green; my own eyes are green; Gable's eyes must have been green) making contact now and again with each member of his congregation. Carter Hays it was who first told me and my brother how the body of an ancient Hudson had come to rest at the bottom of Ely's Sandpit.

Mr. Ely was one of Attica's few rich men. He owned the largest industry in town, the elevator, and during harvest when the trucks lined up all the way from hell to breakfast to dump their grain I often would return to the Champlin station, having hustled the *Beacon*, and sit on the green-slatted bench and watch the wheat spill from the truckbeds into a grate-covered pit, from there to be delivered by auger into one of the three white towering silos. Watching truck after truck spilling its enormous load—grain without end, it seemed to me, grain enough to feed the world and then some—I marveled to imagine how rich old man Ely must be. For starters, he and his wife lived in the largest house in town, an elaborate combination of brick and stone with two blue rounded windows on the third floor rivalling Chartres. In addition, Mr. Ely owned a truckload of acreage outside the city limits, and one of his holdings was a farm two miles due east of town. L. H. Davis, who was also the school superintendent, managed the farm; he was the father of Donna Grace, Queen of Spellers, who sat in the desk at my right in the fourth grade.

A good distance from the farmhouse, near a gravel road, lay the sandpit, small but deep. Mr. Ely owned that pit—and the farmhouse and its outbuildings and the land around it and the mansion in town and God alone knows what else—and sitting on that green bench at the Champlin station, watching a bountiful harvest as if an eternal downpour disappear into the inscrutable machinations of Mr. Ely's elevator, I thought long and hard, as my friend Bill Stafford already has said it, "for all of us."

Carter says that the body of the Hudson lies at the bottom of the sandpit because passion is something that most people have difficulty living without. There was this young and beautiful girl, see, Carter says, and she was in love with this young and handsome boy. One night, he says, his fingers fluttering, *late* one night, he says, the boy and the girl were heading home from a party in town, driving home in the boy's father's Hudson Terraplane. The way home took them past Ely's Sandpit. They were laughing and talking, Carter says, and he had his right hand on her leg and she had her left hand on his, and because in the business of passion one thing leads to another the car wandered too far to the right, struck a bead of gravel raised that morning by a road grader, then somersaulted at a very high speed down and into the center of the pit.

Yes, Carter says, the boy survived. No, he says, the girl didn't. The boy tried several times to free her from her prison there in the front seat, but at last, winded and frantic and wet himself almost to the point of drowning, he gave it up.

Carter goes on to describe more vividly than I care to remember the drowned girl, how she looked as she was finally pulled from the wreckage, her hair, her neck askew, her open mouth, how the operation was conducted underwater because the boy's father refused to salvage the Hudson, and so on. With his long fingers and his emerald eyes Carter embellished the story. By the time he finished, Ely's Sandpit had become a place much too awful to be resisted.

So again we go there, Carter and I and my brother, all of us barefooted, my brother and I wearing only denim jeans, Carter in tan washpants and a white T-shirt. We go there to get out of town. We go to feel the sun above the shoulders and the good rich earth of Kansas under the feet. We go because two of us aren't supposed to. And we go because we want to explore again the body of that mysterious Terraplane.

My brother is fearless and can hold his breath almost forever. He is two years younger than I, his birthday 12 November, the same date that the *Juneau* took its first torpedo. He is nine. I am eleven. Carter is older.

Going somewhere forbidden to do something terrifying has a charm that defies total explanation. Shelley gets at a piece of it when he writes,

> . . . *obedience,*
> *Bane of all genius, virtue, freedom, truth,*
> *Makes slaves of men. . . .*

Somehow my brother and I knew what Shelley v
long before we knew he said it. Our parents—M
cially, whose fear of water was on a par with her '
dug caves—warned us many times against o'

much less into, Ely's Sandpit. But my brother and I would not be slaves; we would have nothing whatsoever to do with *bane,* which at that point in our careers we knew as *obedience.*

So under a high August sun we bask and we dip in Ely's Sandpit. Carter tells us again the story of the Terraplane and its lovely unfortunate victim. I hold my nose and kick myself downward until with my free hand I can feel first the top of the Hudson, then the hood all the way to where its ornament would be if someone hadn't stolen it. Shortly before my lungs explode I break the water's surface, gulping then the sweet ambience of oxygen.

It is one of those summer days in Kansas when the sun doesn't move — perhaps because there isn't any wind to move it, perhaps because of its own stifling heat, perhaps because it has a mind of its own and doesn't want to. The water in Ely's Sandpit is unusually clear; now and then I see a carp moving slowly and securely, as if a peacetime submarine, in the direction of moss. Now there's another element of potential disaster, that carp and its brethren: swimming naked, I want no part of me to be misconstrued as bait.

Did I mention that my brother is a daredevil? Don't draw a line and challenge him to cross it unless you have your fists closed and cocked. He is not overtly aggressive; he laughs easily and frequently, and should he live a long, long time he might one day grow a mouth sufficient unto his middle upper teeth. He has no quarrel with the world; he is instead a Renaissance young man, yearning to try everything and to perform to perfection everything he tries.

He had been the first one into the water; he hit it at a gallop, his little pecker swinging like a metronome. Once into

the laving liquid of the sandpit, my brother as a rule doesn't leave it until we head for home. He swims cleanly and without apparent effort; he dives and disappears and emerges sleek as a dolphin.

Even today my brother can hold his breath forever. That August afternoon at Ely's Sandpit he held it perhaps a bit too long, even by his own admission. He had dived deep under, he said, to explore again the Hudson, and decided this time to swim through a window and seat himself behind the wheel to drive that sorry Terraplane—how far? From town to Timbuktu? From hell to breakfast?

My brother's account of this voyage was an epic worthy of Homer or Virgil or, more appropriately, of Dante or Melville. For my brother had descended into a watery inferno and survived to tell.

So he told it, in more detail than I care to recount, as Carter and I took turns carrying him across an ocean of wheat stubble back into town. He had cut the artery, he believed, on a shard of window glass on the passenger side of the Hudson after he had done his touring and was leaving the vehicle to return to the realm of the finless to resupply his oxygen. He hadn't realized how deep the gash was, or how wide—thus he had waited until the last moment to call for help. At that time, my nine-year-old brother was not much bigger, as our mother often said, than a minute (why a *minute*? Why not at least an *hour*?), but each of his molecules, from his blond hair down through his oversized teeth to his flat feet, was both animated and fearless, if not downright foolhardy.

I could scarcely believe that such a small body might contain so much blood. Carter had heard his call for help and had believed it; in an instant he was in the water, his arms and legs churning in a chaotic tandem—rudder and paddlewheel explosive and seamless—and almost before I knew what was going on Carter had my brother on his stomach, draining him with one hand against his back and with the other applying pressure to the most relevant point.

Much of Ely's Sandpit was a wake of redness, a red snake gorging itself on water until finally the snake would turn to pinkness, eventually then to be taken in, purged and colorless, by the very water it had fed on.

True redness meanwhile came in spurts from my brother's foot whenever Carter released the pressure. *Artery.* And *spurt.* Those words no less than *Stuka* and *Zero* and *sortie* are magic, my brother's blood one of two rednesses by which I have come to measure all redness.

That voyage across a sea of stubble, now that I view it from the other end of the telescope, appears too archetypal to be passed over lightly. Observe this: my little brother, whiter than any lily, but undaunted, yielding himself to the older arms of our buddy and mentor, Carter Hays. Observe this: long fingers on Carter's right hand pressing from time to time that crucial blood-flow point on my brother's lower body. And this: my brother's older brother in lock step with his companion, clodhoppers kicking dust and stubble as he listened to the victim's account of his own private voyage in the Terraplane.

Well, didn't Odysseus spend much of his life on water, water to take him away, water for his return? Didn't Aeneas carry his father Anchises safely away from the burning and toppling towers of Ilium? Didn't Dante experience the considerable swirl and spurt of redness (consider for example the plight of

32

the suicide) on his descent into perdition? Didn't Ahab, that splendid monomaniac, finally confront more water than he had bargained for?

With Carter beside me doing most of the carrying I walked across one mile, then another, of dry south-central Kansas earth, above us a sun that had cast off from its moorings and in all due time would send shards of red and pink and aqua, then blue into purple, then purple into purple-black, then black, up and away from a perfectly flat horizon.

We meanwhile trudge along, Carter and my brother and I. Against his ankle my brother's red blood is infinitely thick, profoundly red, remotely lovely, his story as real as any account, ancient or otherwise, that might never have happened.

The other color by which I measure redness came to me first by way of my maternal grandmother's seed catalogs. All of the colors in those catalogs were shiny and distinctive, but red jumped off the page more immeasurably than did any of the others. Phlox and tulip and petunia: my brother's blood to the contrary notwithstanding, how on God's green earth could any red be as red as these? Well, none could—not really. But these reds were in catalogs, and catalogs are devised by man, and man has been known to cheat. These flowers, then, are only pictures of flowers, and the pictures, having been doctored by man, who has the potential for cheating, especially where money is involved, do not accurately reflect the actual flowers.

Or so I believed—until I saw with my own eyes the fruits of my German grandmother's labor: phlox and tulip and petunia budding and blooming in little gardens beside the house, among the yellows of crocus and jonquils and the whites of periwinkles and snowballs, all budding and blooming their primary colors with a three-dimensional distinctness to put to shame the catalog's emaciated one dimension.

Though I had grown up spring into spring looking at my grandmother's shrubs and flowers, I had not truly seen them until shortly after the bombing of Pearl Harbor, and had not truly appreciated their redness until after the spurtspurtspurt of my brother's artery on the shore at Ely's Sandpit.

Not long after the declaration of war, rumor reared its ambiguous and fascinating head. Soon the Japanese would attack our mainland. Soon we would hear overhead the roaring of enemy aircraft, would see the blood-red circle beneath the wing, sun after rising sun. Even now, we whispered, many of the Japanese among us, American citizens from birth, are reverting, are scheming to overthrow our government and thus must be incarcerated—so bring on whatever it takes to shape a prison, roll after ungainly roll of concertina.

In my little town my grandmother's voice was alone in its German accent; it is no wonder that my colleagues in the fourth and fifth grades managed to allow me to overhear them: *Anna Yock is in cahoots with the Gestapo. Willie's grandma sends codes in letters to the Third Reich. Whose side is she on, anyway? Krauthead!*

In daylight I didn't believe them. But at night, in bed with my small brother, my brother asleep, I could not resist wondering. Grandmother did indeed have an accent—a thick one to those who didn't know her very well—and she did speak often of writing letters to her relatives. She had come to America when she was seventeen, her older brother Jake having preceded her, and before her visit ended she met William John, an older man up from working in the Texas oil fields, and passion like one of her later red petunias bloomed and she never returned to the old country.

And, too, my grandmother was a somewhat selfish and opinionated woman—pig-headed, her own daughter (and perhaps her two sons also) sometimes called her, and who could argue? She was a wide, thick woman, and had she been six inches shorter she would have been square—especially when she went barefooted, or wore her brown cotton hose in lieu of shoes, hose with the stubs of her dark toes showing. It came to this: if she liked you, she could not like you enough. If she found fault with you—and she was a detective of the first order— she would either ignore you or, if the occasion presented itself, would speak to you with unkind words inflected unkindly.

Because I am committed to Truth I must tell it: I was her favorite grandchild. And why shouldn't I have been? Each day, for free, I delivered her a *Beacon*. Each Sunday I took her to Sunday-school and stayed for church. Time and again, at her insistence, I kicked off my shoes (to humor her, of course: she was always the first to wrench her feet from her black undersized dressups) and remained for dinners-for-two that never ended: homegrown peas or string beans (in season, that is, corn otherwise), mashed potatoes, thick dark gravy (the chunk of beef having been deliberately over-braised), hot rolls, iced tea, and a Gargantuan wedge or so of chocolate banana pie.

One Sunday in particular I remember. We had gone to church and had heard the minister tell us to guard against laying up treasures on earth—an admonition that near-indigents liked to hear because it was one road, at least, that we

35

had no trouble traveling—and had returned to Grandmother's, where I had earlier committed myself to staying for dinner.

The ritual, an extension of the Communion we had observed in church, went smoothly: Grandmother wrenched off her shoes, then tied on an apron, a large square of white cotton with a red rooster embroidered at the center, and I kicked off my spit-shined lowtops and occupied a chair at the kitchen table. My task, twofold: (1) keep out of the way; (2) tell stories, ask questions, say anything to keep the conversation going.

I was doing both, and in the process watching Grandmother stretch as high as shortness permits to bring down a platter from a shelf in the cupboard, when suddenly she lost her balance and dropped the platter, and because it must have struck the linoleum precisely wrong it shattered like a clay pigeon taking a bull's-eye.

For the longest time Grandmother looked down at the demolished platter. When finally she looked up, I could see tears large as marbles descending from the cataracts on her eyes.

Later she will tell me about the platter, how it had accompanied her all the way from the old country, from her parents' little farm near Karlshuld, how it was not really an expensive piece—flawed Dresden china—but how nonetheless it mattered, it being the only genuine memento from the homeland to survive the years, to survive Grandfather even, dead before I was born, and so on.

When I moved to help her, Grandmother shook her head. Then she began to laugh, her false teeth clicking like little castanets. She stood there in the midst of her shattered memento, weeping and laughing at the same time, her hands and her brief arms lost behind the intricate stitching on her red-rooster apron. She had wanted to make this near-Easter Sunday more special than ever by serving the chunk of roast beef on her sacred platter, and maybe she was laughing now because she was remembering what the preacher had said about the laying-up of earthly treasure: Don't do it. Well, she had done it, had hoarded away her piece of flawed Dresden china, and now her God was demonstrating the awful righteousness of his awful hand—and maybe that is what my short wide thick gray-haired square-faced unshod German grandmother was thinking as the tears fell and the laughter with its little castanets shook the kitchen.

Then: "I made the mess," she said. "I'll clean it up." In a moment she was back with a dustpan and a broom.

The dinner was terrific. I was ready for it. I had had only a glass of chocolate milk for breakfast, and the Communion at church had been only a tease. I gulped the iced tea *(This is my blood)*; I devoured the roast beef and the peas and the potatoes *(This is my body)*; I drooled over the chocolate banana pie *(This is my grandson, in whom I am well pleased)*.

So there you have the two sides of my conflict, for a long time each balancing the other as if equal weights at the ends of a teeter-totter. At one end: my buddies' rumors, my grandmother's accent, those letters the old woman spoke so frequently of writing—but to whom, really? Relatives? The Gestapo? The Third Reich? Himmler? Adolph himself?

At the other end: my grandmother's flowers fully in bloom, Grandmother home from church sacrificing the last of her earthly treasures to please and to impress her darling grandson.

Simple arithmetic, I believe.

I add: rumor + accent + letters. I record the sum.

I add: flowers + church + platter. I record the sum.

I place one sum at one end of the teeter-totter. I place the other sum at the other end. I stand back to record the difference, if any, between them.

The difference, as it turns out, is enough to vindicate my grandmother. She is not, and has never been, in cahoots with any of the Axis elements whatsoever.

The flowers are the deciding factor. Collectively they quiet rumor, subdue accent, cancel letters; individually they approve church, confirm sacrifice. But chiefly they adore, they damn near worship, redness: red phlox, red petunia, red tulip, red geranium. Bright sunlight on this redness makes it impossible to believe that the hand that planted it and nourished it extends to anything or anyone truly committed to malevolence. Simple arithmetic—or perhaps, more accurately, rational theology.

Walking that vast and stubbled field between Ely's Sandpit and the downtown office of Dr. Montzingo, where my brother's narrative of driving a Terraplane underwater will finally end and the stitching up of his wound begin, I see the oozing and the occasional spurting of blood so closely related to my own and I think of all that redness budding and blooming in my late grandmother's clay pots and galvanized tubs and manicured gardens.

"Rose," asks Kenneth Koch in one of his book titles, "where did you get that red?"

Until a better answer comes along, I'll settle for this: from the hand of my German grandmother.

No true Kansan ever does anything the easy way.—Kansas folklore

Drink waters out of thine own cisterns,
and running waters out of thine own well.
—Proverbs 5:15

It's true: you don't miss the water until the well runs dry.

I learned this from my paternal grandfather, who I believe learned it himself from a quarter section of hill and rock and gumbo in southeastern Kansas.

He had farmed a more productive quarter section just north of my hometown, but lost that section for some reason or other and was forced to settle for whatever he could afford, which then was next to nothing. I am certain that the man he bought it from had given it up as a lost cause. Occupying a scraggly chunk of Chautauqua County southwest of Cedar Vale, this farm had precious little to recommend it—except perhaps its price. But my hard-handed grandfather and my tight-lipped grandmother moved their mortal necessities into an unpainted cracker box on the side of a hill and began their lives as tillers of the soil all over again.

Both house and outbuildings were equally run down—lopsided granary, chicken house with chicken-wire windows askew, an open-faced lodgepole barn, a ramshackle two-holer outhouse with a maverick osage orange sprawling above it, in season dropping its fruit dense as cannonade onto the shake-shingle roof. I tell you, to make use of this facility was an exercise in high and terrifying adventure—a sensory barrage in a vertical dinghy moored on an inland sea. "The ripeness," Shakespeare says—"the ripeness is all," though the context he states this in is somewhat removed from my grandfather's two-holer outhouse. Nebraska philosopher-scientist John Janovy contends that certain roadkills at certain moments provide, in the hands and at the nose of the empirically curious, the ultimate in olfactory sensations; but Janovy did not serve time on the pine splinters of C. A. Kloefkorn's privy. And if on occasion one found himself somewhat pleasantly settled in—contemplating, say, the immensities of the universe—an osage cannonball might suddenly detonate on the roof, and any effort at meditation would instantly be over.

Hill and rock and gumbo. Grandfather's one-story house was more connected to than built on the side of an intimidating hill, and the hill was anything but an anachronism, Chautauqua County being comprised of hundreds of hills just like it. The house's foundation was made of local stones, none of them, I think, cut to fit, all heavily and crudely mortared. Along the west side of the house, that side abutting the hill, a line of stones one stone deep served as foundation; along the east side of the house a vertical of more than a dozen stones served to level the foundation from east back to west. A porch on stilts had been joined along the east side, but no steps had been provided. A door from the living room opened onto the porch, and if you wanted off the porch but did not want to use the door you had two options: jump (and try to avoid hitting a rock below) or shinny down one of the stilts.

Two other porches: one, an excuse for a place to stack the firewood, ran like an abbreviated boardwalk from the kitchen screen door at the center of the north side of the house to the northwest corner, its pyramid of firewood somewhat protected by an overhang of one-by-sixes overlaid with corrugated tin. The other porch, at the south side, was screened in and its floor, though unpainted pine, was made of one-by-fours tongue-and-grooved. This porch was magic.

I do not disagree with Eiseley: *If there is magic on this planet, it is contained in water.* But there is magic in other liquids, too, perhaps chief among them cow's milk. My grandfather's south porch contained both.

He had dug a deep hole beneath the porch and lined it and somehow connected a truckload of subterranean downspouts to it; thus when rain fell, it coursed and curved and sloshed its convoluted way down into the cistern. *Cistern.* I say it aloud: *Cistern.* More magic. (Mother, recalling that afternoon at Simpson's Pond: "Your father rolled you onto your stomach and pumped water from you like you were a cistern.") To protect this water, and perhaps any children who might be unduly curious, Grandfather had provided a lid for his cistern, a sawed-out circle of pinewood porch about three feet in diameter, that he attached to the porch floor with a large hinge. This lid, then, with a weight and a rope and a couple of pulleys, could very easily and conveniently be raised and lowered. A longer rope, and a larger one, both ropes fraying hemp, he attached to a five-gallon bucket that he kept very neatly at the center of the lid. If you need water to fill the reservoir at the side of the kitchen range—water to be heated by the wood fire in the range, water then to be dipped out for washing hands and faces and dishes—you do the following:

1. remove the bucket and the rope from the center of the lid;
2. raise the lid by forcing down the weight at the end of the pulley-rope;
3. lower the bucket until you see its bottom strike water;
4. jiggle the bucket until it turns onto its side;
5. jiggle further until the bucket begins to fill;
6. give the bucket its rein, permitting it to fill completely;
7. raise the bucket carefully and slowly;
8. grasp firmly the handle of the bucket and place the bucket on the porch floor;
9. lower the lid by raising the weight; and
10. empty the bucket into the reservoir, returning it then to the center of the lid, winding the rope around it as if you had spent some time in the United States Navy and therefore know what the hell you are doing.

Add to these steps this rule, if you are a child: Don't ever raise the lid without a grownup present.

But doesn't obedience enslave us? Isn't obedience the "Bane of all genius, virtue, freedom, truth"? On many occasions, the coast clear, I raised the lid to lie on my stomach to look down into the reflective mystery of Grandfather's hand-dug cistern. If I looked long enough, and I almost always did, I could sense the house slightly moving, whereupon cistern turned to pond, pond to lake, lake to ocean, and I was belly-down at the center of it, its liquid eye doing its liquid best to stare me down. Already I had toppled into Simpson's Pond; before long Jackie

42

Dellman would be standing at the cloakroom window weeping, his hands forming fists at his sides, the flesh of hundreds of young men trapped within the *Arizona* twenty-four hours on its way to becoming bone.

But at the moment I was looking into a damply aromatic opening that seemed to have no end. I would roll to one side to reach into a pocket to bring forth my secret weapon—a handful of small rocks gleaned from anywhere on the acreage—and one by one, long intervals in between, I'd drop them, trying to pinpoint each landing at what seemed to me the precise center of the cistern. (Wouldn't it be the Norden bombsight that would give the Allied forces the advantage of pinpoint bombing?) I would aim a rock, drop it, note its impact (first sound, then sight, small circles encircled by the cistern's concrete lining), wait until the surface returned to an absolute blue-black smoothness, then drop another rock in. Only fear of being discovered by a grownup kept me from being there yet.

But there is magic in other liquids, too, perhaps chief among them cow's milk.

On the same porch beneath which the water of a cistern ebbed and flowed sat the cream separator, an apparition worthy of Pablo Piccaso: in the early rays of morning it looked like a one-armed creature with a bulbous head and two silver extrusions, one for the delivering of cream, the other for the delivering of milk. *Milk.* The word is one of the few monosyllables in our language that all by itself flows. Everything related to this word, remote or otherwise, connotes favorably.

Visiting these grandparents over a weekend in summer, or

in December, before Christmas, I would not go to bed until Grandfather promised to wake me so that I might help him with the chores. I would arise groggily, heroically, from my bed, and under a surprising confederation of stars I would accompany him across a back yard eerie with budding boulders to the granary for a bucket of grain, to the cow lot where half a dozen Guernseys stood chewing their cuds, to the stanchions beneath the lodgepole barn where the cows would form a dutiful echelon, their large mouths eager to begin slobbering the grain. And I would ask for a milkstool, one short two-by-four nailed to a longer one, and I would sit on the stool and, leaning my forehead against the cow's warm flank, with my right hand I would brush away whatever debris had found its way to one or more of the teats—a sliver of leaf, perhaps, or a splat of dried manure—and I would squeeze one teat in each hand, chiefly between the thumb and the forefinger at that place where teat joins udder, then firmly but gently pull downward, delivering alternate streams into a silver bucket I tried my best to hold between my knees. And when the cats with their kittens gathered, as they always did, I would treat their mouths to an occasional jet of white warm milk. My grandfather at the flank of his own cow did the same thing.

Sounds of early morning: the hiss of milk against the side of a silver pail; the bawl of a calf muted but intense from a distant pasture; the whirr of a cream separator rising to a steady soprano, Grandfather's freckled hand turning and turning the arm that Picasso might have devised—the handle. Standing on unpainted one-by-fours not more than a dozen feet from the lid of the cistern I would watch my grandfather turn the handle, watch the thick cream spill downward from the trough of one obtrusion, watch milk white as a bedsheet spill downward from the other. *If there is magic on this planet . . .*

I came into this world trailing milk-white clouds of cow's milk. When I was born, my parents and my older sister lived on a farm two miles north of town, a two-cow place they rented from Mr. Broce. Mother, who claims not to be a storyteller, tells the story, how having finished milking the second cow she felt her body going into labor, how she left that second cow unstripped to carry the bucket of milk across the lot and across the yard and up the steps to the back porch and into the house, where she telephoned the hospital at Anthony, leaving word for Dr. Galloway (whose name several years later would be on the lips of Ira Wyrick as he tells my mother that my father, having twisted off two of his fingers, was in the hospital at Anthony. "He's going to be all right," Mr. Wyrick says. "He's under the care of Dr. Galloway"). How Dr. Galloway arrived in time to deliver the baby. How the bill was paid with eggs and chickens and homegrown pork. How the baby weighed 10 pounds and 8 ounces and was, in all honesty, ugly as sin. (Ugly as *sin*? What sin, in particular? And by whose judgment, whose standards?)

When I was two my parents left the farm and moved straightway into town: Mr. Broce decided he wanted the two-cow place for himself. Father bought one of the cows, two of the pigs, and several of the chickens, and we packed our mortal treasures into a shoebox and, having driven our beleaguered Chevrolet over the Sand Creek bridge just north of the city limits, rattling the planks, we set up housekeeping all over again. The town had no objection to our keeping birds and

45

animals. In most respects the town was itself an overgrown farm with a good crop of churches, a couple of filling stations, a depot and a pool hall and a cafe and Mr. Ely's elevator. The chickens, in any case, adjusted without incident, pecking the plentiful Kansas dust, and the pigs in their wiry confinements squealed and lolled exactly as they had squealed and lolled back on the farm.

And the cow or its descendent gave plenty of milk, a quart of which several years later I delivered each day to my grandmother.

Because of this: the Great Depression was hanging on, and my father's work with the county kept the family sufficient but not all that far away from destitute. So for a year my sister went to live with Grandmother, who likewise lived on a shoestring but who somehow managed to do more with her shoestring than we did with ours. Besides, Grandmother was quite fond of my sister and had high German hopes for her: the old woman would teach the young girl how to knit, how to crochet, how to darn, how to put the color (principally red) into phlox and petunia and geranium.

My part in all of this: deliver a quart of fresh milk each day to Grandmother to help defray my sister's expenses.

How peculiar that voyage from my house to Grandmother's! In my hands I hold a quart bottle white with the milk from a cow the likes of which Mother had been about to strip seven years earlier when the labor pains began, milk like the milk I watched descend in a film like a waterfall from the trough of the separator's obtrusion. And the bottle: how precious, how breakable! And how often I could not resist the temptation: holding the bottle firmly by its neck, I would toss it into the air, would practice at one, then two, revolutions. Down the alley and across a street and down the alley again, stopping from time to time to juggle the bottle, stopping almost every trip to watch old man Giggy's minks thrashing in their cages, until having reached another street I'd turn east for one block, then south for two more, then across a shallow ravine and backyard rippling with flowers in season, then up the steps of the back porch and through the back door and into the kitchen.

More often than not my sister would be there to greet me, to take the bottle of milk off my hands. And that, too, was an element of the journey that bewildered and perplexed me. A quart bottle of cow's milk from my hand into the hand of my sister, a young woman who, living no longer at home, seemed suddenly, almost miraculously, a partial stranger, and when we spoke to each other we picked our words with thought and care. At one such meeting, after she had been away for several weeks, I thought I read in her eyes this consolation: *Nothing lasts forever*—though I believe she was happy enough with Grandmother, in spite of her inveterate inability to handle any size or type of needle. Even so, sometimes at night I would go to sleep thinking of my sister, half stranger, crocheting the perfect doily, giving it to me then to decorate the slats of the orange crate I kept beside my bed. On the doily I'd place the glass of milk I'd drink to wash the last of the crackers down before switching off the light. A delicate doily, made of white thread assembled by my sister's fingers in the shape of a star.

When all of the cream had been separated from all of the milk, I would go back to bed, lulled by the sound and the flow and the absolute whiteness of milk. If the month were December, I would remove my coat and cap and overalls, my boots and socks, and crawl onto a featherbed that like the cistern seemed to have no bottom; and in that chilly bedroom I would cover myself with quilts until I could scarcely move.

Smells of early morning: hint of alfalfa in a lingering trace of manure; something akin to a mild breeze in the starch from the pillowcase; moist scent of my own breath entrapped beneath the aging of handstitched quilts; and on the fingers the sweet aftermath of milk. *If there is magic on this planet . . .*

Grandfather worked at trapping water because there was otherwise no running water on his farm—no spigot, no faucet, no showerhead, no shower. Though not impoverished, he was certainly poor; and just as certainly he was stubborn and proud. When he moved from the more productive farm to the quarter section of hill and rock and gumbo southwest of Cedar Vale he took both workhorses and tractor, knowing, I suppose, that the John Deere was on its last lugs. Sure enough, he hadn't been on the second farm very long, rearranging rocks and planting some lespedeza on this slope, some winter wheat on that one, when the John Deere stopped pinging and resisted all efforts (which weren't many) at resuscitation. Without missing more than a beat or two he put the tractor up on blocks and harnessed the workhorses and continued the planting.

He continued also the trapping of water, not only in the form of a cistern, but in the oval shape of a pond.

As a boy I watched him work the horses to level a patch of rock and potential gumbo southwest of the house. I believe now that he was driven fully as much by stubbornness as by indigence: there had never been running water on this farm before, and goaded by some perverse sense of continuity, he would work himself to death to keep the tradition intact. He had precisely the same attitude toward electricity. All around him the REA had planted poles and strung wires and affixed switches, bringing wonder and wattage to farm after farm. But not to my grandfather's. Its darkness had never been doused with anything stronger than the kerosene lamp, and Grandfather would fumble in half-light, would trim wicks and would funnel fuel into lamp after lamp, and Grandmother would wash and dry the shim-thin globes until eternal night descended before they would yield to modernity.

And, too, they had no money.

Having leveled an area large enough to accommodate a pond, Grandfather began to dig the hole. He didn't *dig,* exactly, as with a shovel or a spade. He *scooped,* as with a monstrous iron device called a *slip.* It looked like a Brobdingnagian scoop but was labeled *slip* because at either side it sported a contraption with a heavy spring that permitted the scoop to give way, or slip, should it strike a treeroot or a rock or anything substantial enough to prevent the blade to continue its scooping.

Grandfather held tight to the sliphandles as he worked the team of horses, and I heard as well as observed him — whistling and geeing and hawing, sawing the reins, once in a while in his animation losing his sweatstained gray felt hat, and managing somehow each time to retrieve it without having to disengage himself from either slip or rein. Like my father, my grandfather, immersed in his work, rarely came up for air. (Like my grandfather, my father had little sympathy for

49

indoor plumbing, especially if he had to install it himself. Is it any wonder, then, that Father balked when Mother demanded, even at the implicit request of Providence, an indoor facility?)

Inch by inch, rock by rock, the stubborn Kansas earth gave way to the blade of the slip until an oval depression with its innards for a berm declared itself: *I am pond.*

The declaration proved premature, if by pond one means not only berm and depression, but also water. A brief drought set in, and though I was not visiting the farm when it broke, I remember Grandfather's description. (Memory and hearsay: what I wasn't there to witness, I'll gather from someone else.) When the rains came, Grandfather said, they came with a vengeance, and what he knew of gravity proved sufficient: the waters flowed downhill in dozens of rivulets, zigzagging bunchgrass and rock, until fathom by fathom the depression filled, and the voice of the water saying *I am pond* was heard this time as gospel across the land. Grandfather described the rains and the filling of the pond without wanting to appear or to sound unduly proud, but I nonetheless could detect at least a modicum of self-fulfillment in his eyes: Whatever one builds, shapes, creates with his hands, or with his hands extended, and if the product enriches life, is holy.

When he had arrived at this acreage neither pond nor cistern existed. Thus he, and Grandmother with him, came to know in their bones the meaning, the essence, of water. And through them, I came to know it as something more than a pit or a harbor for human flesh to drown in.

When the rains descended they not only filled the pond (and the cistern also, of course, Grandfather's convoluted system of downspouts working overtime), they concurrently scoured the rocks and the boulders, so that the smaller ones, those made invisible with a long-time coating of dust, seemed suddenly to burst through the sod and bloom—a thousand Athenas appearing from the gumboed earthhead of Zeus. Many of these my grandfather with his workhorses and wagon and a strong back eventually would remove, would use as fencing to augment barbed wire and osage orange, or would arrange in peculiar cairns to bewilder some future observer intent on finding a pattern in rocks and dust and sod.

Then—the land dry, the field for lespedeza plowed and harrowed and ready for planting—a rain would fall, and more rocks from absolutely nowhere would break the soft soil and bloom, these little births occurring even as pond and cistern were filling . . .

Now here is a tale of rainwater and of washtub—and of my paternal grandmother.

I had not been first introduced to either rainwater or to washtub at my grandparents' farm; we had both of these in my hometown. The washtub was the dominant object because it was used with clockwork regularity: in it, I bathed as a toddler every Saturday night, and from it, as a youngster, I poured the water, rinse and otherwise, made grimy with Monday's Maytag washing. I had mixed feelings about the waters in all those tubs. On the one hand I did not like to stop my playing to undress to be lathered and rubbed until my skin turned pink as a peony; on the other hand, having survived, it did feel damn good to be squeaky clean. On the one hand I did not look forward to draining and rinsing the Maytag, to carrying its sloshy and cumbersome contents outside to dump on the buffalo grass. On the other hand, having finished, it did feel damn good to crawl into a clean shirt and affix the snaps on a clean pair of overalls.

At my grandparents' farm I felt no such ambivalence, probably because I encountered a washtub only once, and because that single encounter required no personal effort, no personal sacrifice whatsoever. Instead, it gave me a pleasure that to this day I can neither fully describe nor account for.

All morning that Saturday the rain had fallen; the level of pond and cistern had risen, and the rocks were blooming squeaky clean at their baths. Around mid-afternoon the clouds dispersed as quickly as they had gathered. Under a full high August sun creatures awoke from their dormancy, yawning and stretching, ready now for whatever life might give or bring or yield to make their lives, however full already, more fulfilling.

My grandmother must have been among them. She must have been struck by the sun in such a way, at such an angle, that for the amazing space of half an hour she had no choice but to be that woman she sometimes alone at night had dreams of being.

That morning when the rain began she had set a small washtub on a tree stump in a clearing just south of the south porch. That afternoon, looking myself for something to make my own little life fulfilling, I happened around the southeast corner of the house, that part shaded by the porch on stilts, when I saw it: Grandmother washing her long white hair in rainwater.

Stunned, I retreated back into the shade to watch her, to make certain that what I thought I saw I was yet seeing. I had never imagined my grandmother's hair in such a context, had never seen it except in a high tight bun kept securely in place with half a dozen short curved combs. She was not always a quiet person; in her kitchen she talked and clattered, and though she was small, almost petite, she handled the potato masher as if the jawbone of an ass whose purpose on earth was to annihilate Philistines.

But in most other ways she was a very reserved and private woman, her modesty linked directly, I am certain, to her constricted view of religion. She (Grandfather, too) belonged to an order that believed in not believing: she did not believe in dancing, in drinking, in swearing, or in wearing makeup—nor did she believe in practicing any of these, or any of a hundred other human indulgences, even in moderation. Her stoutest expletive was "Mercy!" Grandfather's was "Pshaw!" I am certain that she viewed even these as crimes of excess, but as tiny ones for which daily prayer might reduce if not entirely dismiss the charges. One more item: she did not believe in most forms of entertainment.

Case in point: the day that she caught me hypnotizing a chicken.

I somehow sensed that this was a form of entertainment my grandmother would disapprove of, so I tried to do it secretly, keeping the ramshackle granary between me and the chicken and the house. I had used a shepherd's crook to snag the leg of the chicken, the same device (#9 wire with a crook at one end and a wooden handle at the other) Grandmother used to catch Sunday dinners. I had caught a fat white unsuspecting hen with my first effort, had replaced the crook on the nail beside the chicken house door, then had chosen an expanse of brown earth at the northeast corner of the granary on which to conduct the entertainment.

Hypnotizing a chicken is not difficult. It requires only a chicken and a small plot of barren ground, and a stick. The method is this: (1) catch the chicken; (2) grasping the chicken fully and firmly in both hands, go to the knees; (3) continuing to grasp the chicken with both hands, force it downward until the entire length of its belly makes contact with the ground; (4) with one hand at the chicken's back to keep its belly against the ground, reach the other hand into that pocket where you earlier stuck the stick and retrieve it; (5) place one end of the stick against the ground immediately in front of the tip of the chicken's beak; (6) begin slowly to move the stick away from the beak, forcing a furrow into the earth as you do so; (7) when the furrow is approximately twelve inches long, begin *very slowly* to raise the stick, at the same time, *and just as slowly,* begin to raise the other hand from the top of the chicken; (8) continue to raise both stick and hand until the former no longer makes contact with the ground and the latter no longer makes contact with the chicken; (9) continue to raise the hands until they reach eye level; and (10) stand up quietly and deliberately, then back away and enjoy the entertainment.

The chicken will remain delightfully immobile, its eyes beady and fixed, for a long time, and how you occupy your own time during the interim is pretty much optional. On that particular Saturday afternoon in August, my chicken beautifully hypnotized on earth dryly aromatic from a layer of fine well-sifted dust, I stood beside and above it, waving the stick as if a choir director as I sang softly

We shall not be, we shall not be moved!
We shall not be, we shall not be moved!
Just like a tree that's planted by the water,
We shall not be moved!

Though I sang softly, I sang with intensity, intensity being something I had learned from attending camp-meeting revivals with my grandparents. And hindsight informs me that when Grandmother happened upon the scene and saw the immobile chicken with me beside and above it, waving a stick and singing a perfectly serious and inspirational Christian hymn, she came quickly to the conclusion that I had moved beyond entertainment all the way into sacrilege and must therefore be punished.

She hustled me into the house and sat me down at the kitchen table and told me not to move until she came back. I didn't. But my mind raced, and wondered. What had she been doing out in the back yard, anyway, so close to the granary? (Later I learn the answer: she had been about to catch her own chickens to behead and dress and put on ice for Sunday dinner.) And why . . .

She materialized beside me, holding in her lean stout fingers her personal copy of the King James Bible. She placed it on the oilcloth and opened it and told me to memorize at least three verses. I would sit there all night, if necessary, she said, until the verses, *word for word,* were committed to memory.

Because I had all night—and much of the day, too, it being only three or four o'clock—I took my time. The King James Bible is a thick book, yet in turning its pages I could find no verses relating either directly or indirectly to the hypnotizing of chickens. Certainly a reference in Psalms to "flying fowl" did not apply, nor did the section of the creation in Genesis wherein God says, "Let the waters bring forth abundantly the moving creature that hath life, and fowl that may fly above the earth in the open firmament of heaven." My hypnotized chicken, so beautifully inert, might have dreamed of flying, but its day-to-day reality was that of a bird landlocked and heavy-bellied, its wings less functional than delectable.

And so it was that I found no reference to the chicken in flight or to the chicken hypnotized, though I did run across a plea for Jerusalem to gather its children "even as a hen gathereth her chickens under her wings"; but otherwise the King James Bible does not seem to care very much about chickens. It prefers birds that live in valleys beside springs, "fowls of the heaven . . . which sing among the branches," meaning birds that make their nests above ground, I guess, as in trees.

You run across some interesting stuff in the King James Bible, especially in the Old Testament. Grandmother did not seem at all concerned that I might discover some of it; she left me with her Bible, dog-eared and fluffy, then trotted off to snag those chickens for tomorrow's dinner.

I did finally memorize three verses, two of which I knew already: "The Lord is my shepherd; I shall not want. He maketh me to lie down in green pastures: he leadeth me beside the still waters." I had known these verses for a long time—knew, in fact, that entire twenty-third chapter of Psalms from which the verses came. But I decided to try them on Grandmother, anyway; I figured that if I preceded them with a verse I hadn't already known (and I knew good and well that her assignment meant *new verses,* not *verses already committed*), I might pull a fast one.

Before I decided on a new verse I ran across a couple of others that bewildered me. One of them was in Deuteronomy, and it goes like this: "He that is wounded in the stones, or hath his privy member cut off, shall not enter into the congregation of the Lord." Did *stones* mean what I thought it meant? Did *privy member*? If so, did it matter then precisely *how* the wounding or the cutting off happened? What if it had been an accident? What if the cutting off occurred because the victim refused to say that he was not a Christian? What if the victim had thrown his body upon a hand grenade to save a buddy? Did Grandmother realize that her book contained such flammable material? If not, why not? Did she read and study only selected portions? If so, why then would she place such material in front of her grandson, who read voraciously— albeit mostly comic books, the Torch and Toro and Wonder Woman especially?

The other provocative verse was in Second Kings: "For the whole house of Ahab shall perish: and I will cut off from Ahab him that pisseth against the wall, and him that is shut up and left in Israel." It seemed that wherever I turned a page and read, someone or something was being cut off—the privy member in Deuteronomy, now "him that pisseth against the wall" in Second Kings. And though I felt sorry for Ahab and his house, I had a genuine and personal affinity for the phrase "pisseth against the wall." I had done such a thing myself, many times, at home and on my grandparents' farm, and it never occurred to me to feel guilty about it—unless at home I got caught. Grandfather himself did it on the farm. I assumed therefore that where the wall is located makes a considerable moral difference.

In elementary school my buddies and I often conducted contests in the bathroom to determine who could stand the greatest distance away from the urinal and still make contact. Does porcelain used in such a manner constitute a wall? If so, I and my buddies were in deep and probably eternal trouble, our whole houses scheduled inexorably to perish.

At last I settled on a new verse to memorize. Perhaps it was no accident that this verse too had water in it: "Drink waters out of thine own cistern, and running waters out of thine own well."

Having obeyed my grandmother's commandment, I closed her Bible and turned my chair so that I might look out the north kitchen window. I saw framed therein Grandmother, a butcher knife in her right hand, beheading chickens that she had tied upside-down on the clothesline. She did her work swiftly and deftly, tossing each head almost demurely to one side, leaving each decapitated chicken to flap its final spasms into the retirement of a dead and bloody weight. She wore no gloves. The blood from the necks of the chickens made crimson mittens of her hands. Her white hair in its bun bobbed rhythmically as she moved from one victim to another.

I knew the ritual: she would boil water in the range's reservoir, then one by one would scald a chicken and pick it clean. And then—shades of Deuteronomy!—would come the cutting-up, and tomorrow then the frying, the chickens meanwhile in bowls in the icebox waiting.

I watched her then beheading chickens no more closely than I watched her now as she bent her little body over the little washtub, soaping then rinsing her hair. In a simple cotton dress not much fancier than a feedsack she went about the washing as if nothing else human existed to surprise or to confront her. The water in the tub, appropriately enough, had arrived directly from her Heaven, unimpeded by tree limb or powerline, undefiled by the soldered tin of Grandfather's downspouts. For a long time she washed and rinsed her long white hair, and for a long time I didn't move so much as a molecule as I watched her. The white hair reached well below her shoulders, and as she began to dry it with a blue towel the white hair thickened. In brilliant sunlight, her face newly clean, so free of embellishment, so entirely itself, and her white hair long and thickening, Grandmother looked almost like a young girl readying herself for a journey to—where?

To the house, of course, to the three or four steps that would take her to the screen door on the south porch, through it then to the tongue-in-groove floor on which rested the separator and the bucket at the center of the lid on the cistern, thence to the kitchen door beyond which her form, white hair wrapped in a blue towel, would disappear.

When I saw her some time later the hair lay wound on her head in a perfect bun held precisely in place with half a dozen short, curved, this time aqua, combs. Rainwater. Rainwater in a small washtub. Rainwater in a small washtub overflowing in cups that are my grandmother's hands to wash my grandmother's hair. And not all that long ago: Ahab, ah Ahab and your poor beleaguered house, the whole of it a privy member cut off, the whole of it denied forever entrance into the congregation of the Lord. And that other Ahab, his monomaniac bones scuttling the floor of a sea much larger than he bargained for, Ishmael alone surviving to tell the story. They say that time and water sometimes flow uphill, that a fellow once told of a river he saw in Wisconsin that flowed in a circle. Do all of us aspire at last to roundness?

Even after Grandmother had cut up the chickens and had placed their pieces in bowls inside the icebox and then had scrubbed the crimson mittens from her hands, she did not hurry to relieve me. I sat at the kitchen table with her Bible closed in front of me, watching her, wanting to do my recitation so that I might go outside and salvage something from what was left of the day.

When Grandmother at last dismissed me, she did so without mentioning one word about the Bible verses.

I knew, though, that a reckoning would come, sooner or later, because Grandmother had a memory like a schoolteacher. And sure enough, after supper, after Grandfather had trimmed the lamp wicks and filled the lamps with kerosene, after Grandmother had rinsed and toweled the globes, I was invited to take a seat in the living room and with only Grandmother in attendance recite the Bible verses. Actually, I was probably a little too old to be undergoing this sort of pseudopedantic punishment, but Grandmother either didn't know this or, knowing it, chose to ignore it.

I believe now that she chose to ignore it—that she used her form of punishment as a means of being alone with me for a few minutes, and on her own terms. Well, I didn't object at the time, and I don't object now. For one thing, I had committed the verses to memory so deeply that I had no fear of forgetting or stumbling over them. Another thing: during the recitation I was permitted to sit in Grandfather's rocker, a low wide high-backed soft-bottom relic that groaned softly like a baby ghoul when you pushed it into motion.

But mostly I enjoyed the way things looked and the way words sounded in lamplight.

In lamplight everything in the room, Grandmother's face included, flickered just a little, and everything took on a slightly yellowed tint. And the flickering and the degree of yellow varied from one moment to the next, because the flame, however neatly the wick had been trimmed, itself varied — now rising a bit, now falling, now burning evenly, now burning in a series of waves or a skyline of uneven hills.

Grandmother held the Bible, her face and the Bible in her small hands yellowed and flickering, but I noticed that when I recited the verses she did not look down at the page, but instead looked squarely at me. Nor did she object to my including those verses from the Psalms; she smiled, in fact, when I spoke them, so I moved forthwith to the verse from Proverbs: "Drink waters out of thine own cisterns, and running waters out of thine own well."

Her smile faded. "Say that one again," she said. "Say it slowly."

When I finished she said nothing, just sat in her own rocker, one much smaller than Grandfather's, one that fit her perfectly, as if in the beginning it had been assembled around her. I had given Grandfather's chair a push with my right foot, had set its little ghoul to groaning. By now the night had begun to take itself seriously, each succeeding gradation of darkness darker than the one before, each in turn heightening the tones of the lamplight. Off in the kitchen another lamp sat glowing; around it at the table with its oilcloth sat the rest of the family, talking quietly over saucers of dessert.

We sat there for some time, Grandmother and I, saying nothing, rocking. I could see us, or parts of us, in the lamp's lighted globe, and the reflections were a funhouse of distortions. But I did not laugh. Cheeks puffed, necks elongated, mouths fearfully wide—the images were far too eerie to be laughed at. And I knew also that the globe reflecting those images was hot as—hell, maybe. Maybe, if there is a hell, it will be as hot as that lamp globe, and if hypnotizing a chicken might land me there it behooves me just now not to smile. Once upon a time I had placed a hand firmly against such a globe, and when I jerked the hand away much of its skin remained on a curve of glass, sizzling.

Then I heard something, then something else. Enchanted by the images in the lamp globe, I could not at first distinguish between them. But when I looked from the globe to Grandmother, I could see her lips moving, and listening closely I could hear the words. She was reciting some verses from what I much later identified as Ecclesiastes—a time to rise up, and a time to lie down, and so on. Then with another part of me I distinguished the other sound: rain.

Soon I could hear the rain gathering in Grandfather's downspouts, could hear a gurgling as the water moved helter-skelter toward the cistern. And what I could neither see nor hear I could imagine: rainwater giving birth to another generation of rocks, rainwater in rivulets flowing frantically down the hillside and into the pond, there to be taken in by the cows whose milk would pacify the cats, would pacify us all, having dropped from silver troughs on the separator into the silver pails beneath them, in its own inscrutable way becoming the milk in the bottle I delivered each day to a different grandmother, my sister beside her with big eyes saying *Nothing lasts forever,* rain-water that come next summer would fall straightway from Heaven into a galvanized washtub, there to be lifted by the cups of my grandmother's hands to become the santification of her long white hair.

Now because of the rain I could not hear what Grandmother was saying, Ecclesiastes or otherwise. I looked again at the lamp globe. Grandmother's eyes were at mine, her lips because of the flame more tinted than I had ever seen them. And though her words were muted by the rain, her lips were moving.

Then shall the lame man leap as an hart,
and the tongue of the dumb sing. — Isaiah 35:6

Then one morning two and one-half decades later (a blue-sky, early December, windless, almost balmy morning) I found a note on my desk advising me to call Father So-and-So at St. Patrick's Church in the northeast section of Lincoln, Nebraska, where I lived then and almost still do. I had never heard of Father So-and-So, had never been inside St. Patrick's Church, though I knew where it was — three blocks south and one block west of Rohrig's Beverage Mart. And I had never been, and am not now, Catholic, and becoming one is not on my itinerary. But the tone of the note, apparently copied verbatim by the department secretary, sounded somehow both urgent and a trifle personal, so I went directly to the phone.

Soon I was in my desert-tan-under-ivory Bel-Air Chevy headed for St. Pat's. I yet didn't know what the Father wanted to discuss, but his voice had reflected the same tone of urgency I thought I had detected in the note — and because I like to think I'm a reasonable hand at deciphering tone I arranged to talk with Father So-and-So early that temperate afternoon.

He met me at the front step and with a smile and the sweep of his right arm he encouraged me into the vestibule. He was a slight elderly man with a crew cut, gray hair thick and flat as a runway. He wore black with the traditional white collar, and on his feet were brown sandals that I swear did not touch the floor as, gliding across the foyer, he led me into his study. He had introduced himself when he met me at the front step, but already I had forgotten his name. Watching him slip as if weightless across the vestibule, I dubbed him "Father Lightbody."

Father Lightbody showed me to a large straight-backed leather-padded chair, then took for himself a chair much like mine, but at least two sizes larger, behind a desk cluttered with papers and praying hands and crucifixes. He tugged the chair forward until he could rest his elbows more or less comfortably on the desktop, then cleared his throat and smiled. Already I noticed that he smiled frequently and easily, though the smile seemed more automatic than natural, as if the result of a secret button having been pressed—and whoever did the pressing did it, I thought, arbitrarily, often at a moment of high seriousness. This I learned as our conversation proceeded. I learned, too, thanks to his smiling, that he probably smoked heavily, his teeth as yellowed from tobacco as they were ground down from age if not anxiety.

Because I knew not what the hell was going on, I gave Father Lightbody a loose rein. Well, he wanted to know, was my name indeed such-and-such? Yes, I said, indeed it is—but without the "Dr.," I having not yet finished my dissertation on Ernest Hemingway. And do I teach, he continued, at such-and-such university? I pled guilty.

He asked these questions, and several others equally innocuous, as he looked down at the desktop, as if he were taking the questions from a prepared script—as I'm sure he was. He kept touching the fingertips on one hand to the fingertips on the other.

And do you, he asked, looking at me for the first time, have any brothers or sisters?

Now suddenly I felt a slight twinge of fear. Did Father Lightbody somehow know something about my family that I didn't know? Was my sister in danger? Was my brother? And if either was, how the deuce did Father Lightbody know about it?

One sister, I said, who is two years older than I (and who, I did not add, is precisely the sister one might send for if one could send for a sister), and one brother, two years younger (and who, I did not add, not only had had a brush with drowning two and one-half decades ago, but who characteristically outdid his older brother by damn near bleeding to death, too).

Father Lightbody looked back down at his script. I couldn't actually see that he had a script, but I could sense it. Then he looked up and something pushed the smile button. My guess is he went through at least two packs a day.

Does your brother, he wanted to know, teach at a university in Colorado?

His smile, though automatic, had somewhat relieved me: if my sister or brother were in life-threatening danger, or had undergone a truly serious injury, no type of smile, push button or otherwise, would have been even dimly appropriate.

Now the field of two had been narrowed to one: my brother. And though I inferred that he was not in mortal danger, I nonetheless wondered if he might be in trouble to a lesser degree.

Then suddenly the questioning returned to the apparently innocuous: Do I have a family? How many children? What are their ages? Their names?

Then: Does my brother have a family?

I began to smell, ever so faintly, a rat.

Yes, I said, he does: a son and a wife, the latter with whom he no longer lives.

I was surprised not only at what I was saying but with how I was saying it; I detected in my own diction and syntax a formal and official quality that made me wonder if maybe I weren't speaking lines in a second-rate play written by a second-rate playwright. And were the lines saying too much? Shouldn't one of them state, "Go straight to hell, Father—I'll see you later"?

But I was too intrigued and too curious, and maybe too weak-spirited, either to invite Father Lightbody into perdition or to stand up and walk out.

Back and forth the questions bounced—from the mundane and the obviously irrelevant to those related obliquely if not directly to my brother.

I have always been a slow learner, a more or less perpetual sophomore, so it took a long time for the faint smell of rat to become thickly odious. But I began to inhale cautiously when Father Lightbody turned the questioning in the direction of religion—or, more specifically and accurately, church affiliation.

No, I said, in response to a question with church in it, I dropped my affiliation several years ago.

And the church I dropped?

Middle Protestant, I said. It began as United Brethren, then became Evangelical United Brethren, then was absorbed lock stock and barrel by the Methodists.

I could feel my own unofficial voice returning. It felt good. But I still wondered whether I might not be divulging more than I should. The smell of rat was becoming effluvium.

And my brother?

Same church, I said, but always, I added, a much looser connection. He never officially dropped the church, I said, because he never officially picked it up. I liked that, so I smiled.

This seemed to please Father Lightbody, too; someone quickly pushed his smile button, and for a moment we sat in perfect ecumenity, swapping smiles.

Then: *Middle* Protestant? the Father asked. What do you mean, *middle*?

I mean, I said, neither high nor low, Episcopalian and Presbyterian being high, Baptist and Pentecostal being than which there is no lower. I liked that, so I smiled.

Father Lightbody only nodded.

So, he said finally, your brother was not officially a member of your church?

I don't know, I said. I don't remember what if anything we did to make our membership official. Sign a card, maybe. I don't know.

I see, said the Father. He smiled quickly, then dropped just as quickly into a frown.

So he might have been an official member? he asked.

Might have been, I said.

But, said Father Lightbody, you said earlier that your brother never officially *picked up* a church connection.

Yes, I said, but what I meant is that my brother never took the church to heart, regardless of whether or not he signed a membership roster. My brother was a maverick.

This seemed to satisfy Father Lightbody. He made several short sweeping motions then with his right hand, as if to signify a change of focus.

And you, he said, you were at one time a member of the Methodist Church, but you dropped your affiliation?

I dropped it, I said, before my church, the Evangelical United Brethren, was taken in by the Methodists.

The Father smiled. I see, he said. There was a long pause; I could tell that Father Lightbody was girding his loins for something perhaps apocryphal. Even so, when it came I chastised myself for not having seen it coming earlier.

Have you been baptized?

Eventually, of course, after some additional detours and circumlocutions, the question would pertain to John: *Has your brother been baptized?*

Now I not only smelled the fullness of the rat, but I likewise deduced the direction from which the wind of its fullness was blowing. My brother had been seeing a young woman, beautiful and Catholic; I had not met her, but I had heard my brother speak of her, and though he spoke highly he had never mentioned marriage. Perhaps, without keeping his older brother informed, he had decided to indulge the plunge. Or perhaps he hadn't, not officially, and the young woman, believing that sooner or later he would, had gone to her priest somewhere in the wilds of Colorado for instruction and advice. And she had told him many things, among them that John had an older brother who might know more about John than John himself knows—especially about the crucial subject of baptism. I am doing some guessing here, of course. I do not pretend to understand the sensitive and complex machinations that undergird any corporation with a membership of more than a handful.

Father Lightbody repeated the question: *Have you been baptized?*

I could sense that he did not want the question to sound like an accusation, so he asked it softly—then smiled.

I saw an opening and decided to take it; I would delay the other question, the truly pivotal one—*Has your brother been baptized?*—as long as possible.

Yes, I said, I was both sprinkled and baptized, and before Father Lightbody could ask another question I launched first into an explanation of sprinkling, then into a detailed account of the baptism. I was curious: how long would Father Lightbody listen before interrupting?

You see, I said, my baptism was very unconventional. It took place out-of-doors, in a small creek, Shannon's Creek, south of town. Much of the time there wasn't any water in the creek, but that particular summer had been an unusually wet one and Shannon's Creek—Sand Creek, too—was up. But that isn't the principal reason I was baptized there. The principal reason was Oscar Koeppen.

Oscar suffered from severe aphasia and debilitating arthritis, I said. He spent most of his hours in a wheelchair and some of that time in my parents' cafe, which was long and narrow and had a pinball machine without flippers that I could cheat by lifting it onto my toes. Oscar could manipulate his arms and his hands and his fingers sufficiently to manage a hot beef sandwich, say, or a cheeseburger, but he had difficulty with a cup of hot coffee. So I would help him, if I weren't off somewhere else—in the pool hall or the drugstore or folding the *Beacon* in the Champlin station.

Father Lightbody's mouth was slightly ajar. He was studying me as if he were about to reverse his position on transmogrification, if not evolution. I had come into his study in the form of a sane and reasonable Homo sapiens in his mid-thirties and had somehow reverted to become the likeness of a jibbering primate.

Oscar, I hurried on, attended the United Brethren Church; you could find him there every Sunday morning and every Sunday evening, he and his wheelchair out of the way against the back wall. What do you suppose went through his mind as he listened to the minister speak of grace and forgiveness and the prodigal son?

I paused to give Father Lightbody an opportunity to answer. He said nothing.

Oscar Koeppen, I said, could manage not only a hot beef sandwich or a cheeseburger, but he could manipulate a pencil well enough to make himself understood. Under the counter at the cafe I kept a large tablet expressly for Oscar's use. He would pass me notes like a sneaky schoolboy — nothing elaborate, or deep, just "Nice day" or "Feeling fine" — Oscar's scrawl shaky and sometimes so large he had to finish the message on the back of the page. Well, one day he was laboring over a note, Oscar in his wheelchair and I on a stool at the end of the counter, when having finished he handed me a page with a word on it that I could not decipher. I turned the page sideways, then upside-down, but I could not make any sense of Oscar's inflated scrawl.

Oscar meanwhile was making gutteral sounds no more comprehensible than the word on the page. I made several guesses at the word; at each of them Oscar shook his head. I might be there guessing yet if my sister hadn't materialized. She took one look at the word, said "Baptism," then returned to wherever it was she had materialized from.

My friend, you see, wanted to be baptized, but he did not want the ritual to be performed in the church. I believe he perceived himself as both nuisance and embarrassment, and because of this he had gone I don't know how many years — he was sixty, I'd say, or close to it — without asking to be baptized. Or maybe he had been baptized as a child and couldn't remember it and wanted it done again. Or maybe he could remember it but it didn't satisfy him, so he wanted the ceremony performed to his own specifications. I don't know. I know only that a long round of questioning led to this: Oscar wanted to be baptized, and he wanted it done in Shannon's Creek.

And he wanted me to be baptized with him.

Now listen, Father: I was stunned. I did not care to be baptized again; I had been both sprinkled and baptized once, and that seemed to me enough. But when through his notes and his noddings, his grunts and his hand signals and the open-mouthed contortions of his lips, Oscar insisted that I be baptized with him, I reconsidered.

Father, you should have seen the sweet fire in Oscar's eyes when I said yes, when I said hell yes, I'll be happy to be baptized with you in Shannon's Creek.

Shannon's Creek with water in it, Father, is truly a sight to behold. It serpentines over gravel brilliant as mica through Shannon's pasture eventually to join Cedar Creek, those streams together then to the Ninnescah and finally to the Republican River. Shannon is not as well-to-do as is Ely, who owns the elevator, but he more than manages. He has an impressive herd of Herefords and two or three Charolais bulls.

From the onset my minister, Father, was elated at Oscar's request. It was the minister, then, who chose the day and the hour, who seemed blessed with foreknowledge, because that Wednesday afternoon in early August seemed created for outdoor baptism—warm and windless, with last night's shower rising damp and aromatic from the bunchgrass.

I sensed that Father Lightbody had somewhat resigned himself to my narrative, but I knew that behind the resignation, behind the small dark eyes that I thought betrayed that resignation, lay coiled like a serpent the pivotal question: *Has your brother been baptized?* I knew also what Father Lightbody wanted me to say: No, Father, he was never baptized. And, come to think of it, he never officially joined the church. I could imagine Father Lightbody smiling at this, smiling his tobacco teeth this time as if the smile were not altogether automatic; I could see him nodding, could hear him say something like, "Then that should make things easier," meaning, I suppose, that if my brother had had no commitment to Protestantism his marriage to the beautiful young Catholic woman might be easier to arrange.

Father, I had a cheeseburger and french fries; Oscar opted for the hot beef sandwich. I sipped at my iced tea and helped Oscar with his coffee. We had barely finished when I saw the minister's black Ford pull up to the curb. I pushed Oscar in his wheelchair outside and the preacher and I helped him into the car. Actually, Oscar could manage by himself, but with great effort; even then, he could not straighten himself, so he had to waddle close to the ground, using his arms like a skier uses poles for balance.

The preacher, Father, was an obese jolly man whose sermons were a lot like most Kansas waterways, neither deep nor wide. I don't believe he cared. He preferred the song to the word; on Sunday nights, in fact, that's all we did—sing. "Shall We Gather at the River?" "When the Roll Is Called up Yonder." "In the Garden." I still know all three verses to "Let the Lower Lights Be Burning." One of my favorites is "Down Deep in the Sea":

My sins have been cast in the depths of the sea,
Down deep in the sea.
So deep they can never be brought against me,
Down deep in the sea.

Isn't that a helluva concept, Father? You take all of your sins and secure them in a gunnysack, say, then affix a flatiron and toss the whole shebang into the sea, into water so deep they can never be brought against you. I try to imagine how deep that might be, Father, but the mind boggles. Anyway, it's a song that the basso profundo loves to sing, because its last notes are maybe almost as low as the seabottom:

Down, down, down, down, down in the depths of the sea—
The sins of the past are all gone at last,
Down in the depths of the sea.

We sang this song as we rode south toward Shannon's pasture and its meandering creek. Oscar strained to bring forth several grunts and a narrow assortment of gutterals, most of them uttered at the wrong times, but nobody, including the cattle near the barbed-wire fences at the roadside, seemed to mind. Before we had finished more than a couple of other hymns we were there.

I had opened and closed a wood-slatted gate so we could drive the black Ford across the pasture to be as close as possible to the creek. Oscar waved off our offers to help him out of the car. He instead sat there in the back seat, undressing himself, until he was naked as a jaybird. This surprised me. I hadn't really given much thought to how the ritual might evolve, but when Oscar without the slightest hesitation undressed himself all the way down to the nubbins I confess: I was surprised. And when I looked at the preacher to catch his reaction my surprise doubled: he too was naked, and before I could say anything—not that I had anything to say—he had turned and was headed for the water.

As I took off my clothes I watched Oscar maneuver himself out of the car and move crablike toward the hole the minister had found for the immersion. Father, it is difficult for me to say precisely how I felt. There in a pocket of Shannon's Creek, up to his knees in a pool of clean clear flowing water, stood an obese man of God, a married man who had no children because his stones had not formed correctly or completely, and moving towards him was Oscar the beloved crab, and viewing it all was a young incorrigible whose midsection, free of its shirt and its shorts, was as white as the underbelly of a channel catfish.

Humility. Until a better word happens along, I'll settle for—humility. I believe that for the first time in my life I knew a moment of absolute humility, and that moment is a touchstone against which I have since measured all humilities.

Oscar hit the water without breaking stride, if you could call it that. I stood at the front of the Ford, my clothes hanging from the hood ornament, and watched the ceremony. Three times the preacher dunked my friend Oscar; three times my friend Oscar came up sputtering and grinning. Hair plastered to his forehead, Oscar Koeppen looked like a gleeful twisted child.

Minnows, Father: a large school of them scattered when I walked into the water. Three times the obese minister dunked me: In the name of the Father, and of the Son, and . . .

And when I came up for the third time I opened my eyes to see that one of Shannon's Herefords had left the herd to observe the proceedings from a closer range—a much closer range, in fact, because the animal's forelegs were in the creek. The cow was looking straight at me, as if she expected an explanation, and though the afternoon was early already her udder was tight with milk.

No one had thought to bring towels, so we stretched out on pallets of buffalo grass and let the sun do the toweling for us. I remember lying there—first on my stomach, then on my back—with my eyes closed, the hot sun making me giddy, and I remember also that I tried to give the Hereford a silent explanation; but the words refused to come sufficiently together. Tell me, Father: how does one explain baptism to an animal whose body transforms grass and grain into the white milk my grandfather and I directed into the mewing mouths of thirsty cats and kittens?

I paused, giving Father Lightbody plenty of time to answer. When he spoke at last, this is what he said: I need a cigarette.

I went with him outside, where not more than a couple of steps from the front door he lit up.

No, I said, my brother was never baptized. And come to think of it, he never officially joined the church.

Even before Father Lightbody finished his cigarette I had decided to lie. So when the pivotal question was asked, I was ready; and if conscience were water, the surface of mine would have been gloriously free of ripples.

Father Lightbody smiled, this time as if the smile were not altogether automatic; then for some time he nodded.

Then that should make things easier, he said, meaning, I suppose, that if my brother had had no commitment to Protestantism his marriage to the beautiful Catholic woman might be easier to arrange.

5

All the rivers run into the sea;
yet the sea is not full. — Ecclesiastes 1:7

Nebraska is an inland sea blessed with the moving waters of many rivers — Big Blue, Niobrara, Elkhorn, Dismal, Platte, Loup.

To know a river first listen closely to those who know a river. Begin, say, with Mark Twain's *Life on the Mississippi;* take to heart what Mr. Bixby tells his cub pilot about learning the multitudinous shapes of the river:

You see, this has got to be learned; there isn't any getting around it. A clear starlight night throws such heavy shadows that, if you didn't know the shape of a shore perfectly, you would claw away from every bunch of timber, because you would take the black shadow of it for a solid cape; and you see you would be getting scared to death every fifteen minutes by the watch. You would be fifty yards from shore all the time when you ought to be within fifty feet of it. You can't see a snag in one of those shadows, but you know exactly where it is, and the shape of the river tells you when you are coming to it. Then there's your pitch-dark night; the river is a very different shape on a pitch-dark night from what it is on a star-light night. All shores seem to be straight lines, then, and mighty dim ones, too; and you'd run them for straight lines, only you know better. You boldly drive your boat right into what seems to be a solid, straight wall (you knowing very well that in reality there is a curve in there), and that wall falls back and makes way for you. Then there's your gray mist. You take a night when there's one of these grisly, drizzly, gray mists, and then there isn't any particular shape to a shore. A gray mist would tangle the head of the oldest man that ever lived. Well, then, different kinds of moonlight *change the shape of the river in different ways. You see—*

Then listen just as closely to what Huck Finn says after he and Jim are separated and the boy at night is desperately trying to spot the raft:

It was a monstrous big river here, with the tallest and the thickest kind of timber on both banks; just a solid wall, as well as I could see, by the stars. I looked away down stream, and seen a black speck on the water. I took out after it; but when I got to it it warn't nothing but a couple of saw-logs made fast together. Then I see another speck, and chased that; then another, and this time I was right. It was the raft.

To know a river don't always worry or fight it. If the channel is sufficiently deep, and you can see no sign of a snag or a sawyer, settle back and contemplate the little immensities of the universe:

Sometimes we'd have that whole river all to ourselves for the longest time. Yonder was the banks and the islands, across the water; and maybe a spark—which was a candle in a cabin window—and sometimes on the water you could see a spark or two—on a raft or a scow, you know; and maybe you could hear a fiddle or a song coming over from one of them crafts. It's lovely to live on a raft. We had the sky, up there, all speckled with stars, and we used to lay on our backs and look up at them, and discuss

about whether they was made, or only just happened—Jim he
allowed they was made, but I allowed they happened; I judged
it would have took too long to make *so many. Jim said the moon*
could a laid them; well, that looked kind of reasonable, so I didn't
say nothing against it, because I've seen a frog lay most as many,
so of course it could be done. We used to watch the stars that fell,
too, and see them streak down. Jim allowed they'd got spoiled
and was hove out of the nest.

To know a river learn as early as possible the size of the river you want to know.

On a two-week voyage upstream from New Orleans to Cincinnati, aboard the *Delta Queen,* I discovered that Twain's Mississippi is too much water for this country boy to wade in. It is a splendid river, and when the fog rolls in, wanting to obliterate it, and the Captain gives the word to cut the steam that propels the paddle wheel, and the boat sits moored in a blind and uncanny silence, you nonetheless can feel the power of the river beneath you as it rocks your boat like a majestic but pitiful toy. You stand portside at the rail not quite believing that anything as nebulous as fog can be so thick, but there it is. And you strain the eyes to see something, anything, that is not gray-white and rolling. Beneath you meanwhile millions of cubic feet of water do not frankly give a damn whether the fog stays or lifts, whether those attempting to see beyond it fish or cut bait, live or die.

Another river I have yet to assimilate is the Mighty Missouri—in spite of what John Neihardt says about it in *The River and I,* an early book as lyrical as many of the Nebraska Poet Laureate's poems.

The Missouri is unique among rivers. I think God wished to teach the beauty of a virile soul fighting its way toward peace—and His precept was the Missouri. To me, the Amazon is a basking alligator; the Tiber is a dream of dead glory; the Rhine is a fantastic fairy-tale, the Nile a mummy, periodically resurrected; the Mississippi, a convenient geographical boundary line; the Hudson, an epicurean philosopher. . . .

But the Missouri is more than a sentiment—even more than an epic. It is the symbol of my own soul, which is, I surmise, not unlike other souls. In it I see flung before me all the stern world-old struggle become materialized. Here is the concrete representation of the earnest desire, the momentarily frustrate purpose, the beating at the bars, the breathless fighting of the half-whipped but never-to-be-conquered spirit, the sobbing of the wind-broken runner, the anger, the madness, the laughter. And in it all the unwearying urge of a purpose, the unswerving belief in the peace of a far away ocean.

Well, maybe. One must remember that Neihardt wrote his book eighty-five years ago, before the Missouri had been somewhat uniformly dredged and contained. His was indeed a pioneer spirit. He built a boat for the voyage, and he and his comrades spent fifty-six days, some of them truly hectic, descending the river. His lyricism was well-earned.

But then or now, uncontained or otherwise, the Mighty Missouri is not a river I want to risk my soul on. Give me the Platte. Give me the Loup.

To know a river spend some time abiding in a cabin beside it, watching it change with the rising and setting of the sun and with the turning of the seasons.

I lived for several months in a cabin near the Platte River between Lincoln and Omaha. I did not suffer greatly. The cabin, though not quite finished, was commodious and well-equipped; it belonged to a friend who graciously loaned it to me. I was writing a collection of poems, *Platte Valley Homestead,* and the cabin gave me both the privacy and the setting I thought necessary for me to complete the book.

I saw myself as a poor man's Thoreau, the Platte River as my Walden Pond. Each Sunday evening my wife, an Aquarius, drove me to the cabin, or up one of the nearby hills as far as snow and ice allowed, and pulling a toboggan loaded with more supplies than necessary I would make my way to the south entrance, where I would unload the gear and make ready for a week of writing and hiking and whittling and reading and Polish sausage cooked to an appropriate crust in the fireplace.

I took occupancy early in January 1981. In a couple of weeks a new specimen would raise his right hand and be duly sworn in as President of the United States, of the midlands, of Nebraska, of Sarpy County, of Platte Vale Ranch, of the cabin that was a part of the ranch and of the stretch of Platte River that now flowed only under ice in subterranean eddies on its way to its confluence with the Missouri at Plattsmouth. The Platte River in 1981 still clung to the broad ill-defined greatness it had enjoyed before the advent of power and diversion dams, and I was there in a cabin beside it not only to read and to write, but also within the context of my fear of and respect for water to cheer it on.

Not much to cheer for, though, during the short chilly days of January. Having unpacked the toboggan, I would take it

out on the river and gather firewood—mostly cottonwood—
that bloomed leafless and plentiful in the grip of the ice. With
a small tree saw I cut the barkless limbs into lengths the width
of the toboggan and stacked them neatly into a pyramid. At
first I did the gathering slowly and deliberately, exercising a
caution that I inherited from my mother: When your life is
on the line all ice is thin.

My mother didn't recite this line precisely, but she recited
its equivalent until recitation became litany. Her greatest fear
was that I or my brother, or both of us, would one day drown
in either Ely's Sandpit or Heacock's Reservoir, the latter being
a deep funnel-shaped pool kept full by a stream fed constantly
by a spring southeast of Heacock's house. But Heacock's Reservoir, unlike Ely's Sandpit, was never an appealing pool in
which to swim. It was muddy and mossy and filled with turtles and bullheads. Even so, it was a splendid place to run away
to, because both turtle and bullhead were amusing to catch
and torment, and because the reservoir was close to the railroad tracks, giving my brother and me the glowing opportunity to hitch rides to and from the pool on slow-moving
freights.

We did this often, during the summer, thanks to the Atchi-
son, Topeka, and Santa Fe Railroad, Panhandle Division.
Mother in her own way knew that we did it, and the knowing gave her something further to worry about. Apparently
the same Providence that told her she deserved an indoor toi-
let could not be trusted to protect her sons—not from water,
not from the iron behemoth that having stopped for a drink
at the station would clickety-clack its way west, gaining speed
mightily and slowly, until by the time it reached Heacock's

Reservoir it was traveling quite fast enough to make jumping off downright energizing. Eastbound freights, those doing a run between Alva, Oklahoma, and Wellington, and needing water, would frequently approach Heacock's Reservoir moving slowly enough so that with a well-calculated jump we could catch the lowest rung of a steel ladder, then pull ourselves up and hang on for dear life as the freight rattled and hissed and swayed its exciting bulk into the station.

During the summer Mother worried equally about the water and the train. During the winter she worried about the ice, because my brother and I and Carter Leroy Hays and sometimes a couple of others walked or rode a freight to Heacock's Reservoir to skate on the frozen pool using our shoes for skates. Always we were careful to test the ice, sounding it, so to speak, with a length of cottonwood or catalpa.

But we could never be cautious enough to assuage my mother's fears, so her litany of warnings never lessened. They bombarded the brain's neocortex, pervading in force the mammalian level, and seeped in abundance into the primordial reptilian core. One day just several years ago, a brilliant day in early March, they emerged instantaneously as the two-ton truck I was a passenger in suddenly swerved to the right and began to navigate the Kuskokwim River in Bethel, Alaska. Don't worry, the driver said, this is our only major roadway until the thaw.

I had arrived in Bethel in an airplane not much larger than the models of Spitfires and Flying Tigers I laboriously glued and pinched and worried together during the war. From the air Bethel was whiteness interrupted irregularly with scrub bushes and the tops of Quonsets and crackerboxes. The one tree in town — the pilot had pointed it out to me as if he were a guide in the Smithsonian — had been topped several years ago by a snow-delirious citizen who wanted something more than a cutting of prickly pear to decorate for Christmas. The town's vigilantes, he said he believed, would have hanged him had they not feared that his weight would break the limb they wanted to hang him from and further diminish the tree.

Small plane or dogsled: those were the options. I had arrived by plane.

My driver had picked me up and had insisted that he show me the town. It looked pretty much the same from the cab of his truck as it had from the cockpit of the plane, whiteness interrupted irregularly with scrub bushes and the sides, rather than the tops, of Quonsets and crackerboxes.

Then all at once he cranked the truck to the right and all at once we were driving on the frozen river — and all at once my mother's warnings erupted from the volcanic recesses of my brain.

Because my catechism must have been obvious — the teeth clenched, the jaw bunched, the hands squeezing the life from the knees — my driver had reassured me: This is our only major roadway until the thaw. Soon I became convinced that he knew what he was talking about. We met other trucks, and several cars and trucks passed us, and he pointed to an ancient four-door Dodge and told me that it was the river's thermometer: When the Dodge begins to sink, he said, it is time to stay clear of the river. And I thought of the old Hudson at the bottom of Ely's Sandpit, of my brother sitting behind the wheel, holding his breath forever, of the journey he said he took and so vividly described as Carter Hays carried him across a sea of wheat stubble, Carter's right hand applying pressure to the precise point each time the artery began to spurt again . . .

So the first time I constructed a pyramid of small dry cottonwood logs on the toboggan I did it with a measure of fear and trembling, though I believed that the ice was easily thick enough to support me, and though I was reasonably certain that the Platte River in January would not be deep enough to expire in unless one were unduly careless.

I pulled the load back to the cabin and with several of the logs I built my first fire. My friend's cabin, as I noted earlier, was neither as lean nor as hungry as was Thoreau's at Walden Pond. But I had not come to this cabin looking for simplicity (though I found some); I had come for quiet and privacy, for a place to browse and loaf and write, and for a place from which to read the river.

Over the winter months and into spring I did all of these. I first established what I hoped might be a workable dichotomy: I would do my reading downstairs before the fireplace, and my typing and sleeping upstairs in the same room, one with sliding glass doors that opened onto a balcony whose height further enhanced the view of the nearby river. (The cabin, I confess, was on its way to becoming a full-blown house. It had electricity and a shower and central heating; on the other hand, it had no stove or refrigerator, and the front room was serving as a storage shed for nuts and bolts and nails and indiscriminate boards, snakes and snails and puppy dogs' tails.) I would do the cooking in an electric skillet or on an improvised grate in the fireplace. At the bedside would rest a coffee pot, a radio, a flashlight, and — because this was all so new to me, and I would be alone — a hatchet for self-defense. I would be prepared for anything.

Except, as it turned out, for the day-to-day, night-to-night impact of the Platte River.

Other elements of the experience varied from tedious to gratifying. Sometimes an afternoon would refuse to end; I would climb to the top of one of the bluffs and plant a limb to watch its shadow to determine the movement of the sun: *was* it moving? Most of the days and weeks, however, passed quickly; I hiked the shoreline, investigated the considerable windbreak of cedar and walnut north of the cabin, whittled walking sticks of sumac and bur oak until my Barlow pocket-knife gave way to an Uncle Henry that yielded to a Buck that succumbed to a Remington that I sharpened until its longest blade very nearly disappeared. By the light of a cottonwood fire (augmented by a three-way bulb in the floor lamp by my easy chair) I read Nebraska authors, intending to put together a course that I yet hope to be given the chance to teach — Willa Cather, Wright Morris, Mari Sandoz, John Neihardt, Bess Streeter Aldrich, Loren Eiseley. When the embers that one day had been trees with roots too deep almost to sound were little more than cat eyes blinking at me from their dwindling bed I would yawn and go upstairs and undress and be thankful for a bed of my own. All the way from Lexington in the western part of the state KRVN lulled me to sleep with its lovely goofy lyrics: *With blood from my body I could start my own still; and if drinkin' don't kill me her memory will.* At night I turned down the thermostat (simplify, simplify) so that I might go to sleep in a chilly bedroom, cozy beneath a plethora of home-stitched quilts. And many nights I drifted off thinking of my grandfather's rock-strewn, gumboed farm, of my going with him to help with the early-morning milking, of the cats and the kittens begging milk, and frequently in the form of a white jet straight as a string receiving it, of my grandfather's freckled hand turning the handle on the separator, of the separator's whirr and the sounds both milk and cream made as they cascaded into their silver buckets. And of my returning to bed to inhale myself into a deep sleep: aftermath of milk, hint of alfalfa in a lingering trace of manure, something akin to a mild breeze in the starch from the pillowcase; moist scent of my own breath entrapped beneath the aging of quilts, and on the fingers the sweet aftermath of milk. *If there is magic on this planet, it is contained in . . .*

Under those quilts in the cabin the aftermath was that of sumac and bur oak, with an occasional wisp of smoke—frequently cottonwood, sometimes walnut—that had followed me across the room and up the stairs and under the quilts, where all of us yielded without arms quite long enough to reach the off button on the radio: *I turned out to be the only hell my mother ever raised . . .*

But chiefly it was the glory, the jest, and the riddle of the river that kept me most of the time enthralled.

Item: chipping out a chunk of Platte River ice for the cooler.

Each morning, after indulging several cups of coffee and before cooking breakfast, I would clear the snow from a small space of river and with my hatchet I would chip away until I had set free a chunk of ice more than large enough to keep the bacon and eggs, and the beer, cold for another twenty-four hours. This chipping of ice became a ceremony that I performed with scrupulous regularity, and for no practical reason, because a single chunk would have cooled the food and drink for two or three days, and perhaps all week. But I enjoyed the ceremony, the chilly, dry-air feel and smell of it, the tenacity with which the chiseled chunk of ice held on, and on, until a decisive swipp! from the hatchet head released it to the slow relentless movement of the water beneath the ice, water that had begun as snowmelt in the Colorado Rockies and had flowed more than three hundred miles across Nebraska before rounding a bend one quarter of a mile north-northwest of the cabin to trickle and flow beneath where I stood holding its predecessor, a square of ice that would replace a smaller square of ice in the cooler.

When I looked down into the hole where the ice had been I thought of Thoreau doing somewhat the same thing, though the ice on Walden Pond must have been much clearer than that on the Platte River, because having brushed away the snow Thoreau looked down through the ice to describe the bottom of the pond and its fish and other creatures that both swam and were suspended therein; and so mesmerized was he with what he saw that he reached this conclusion: "Heaven is under our feet as well as over our heads."

True. But Hell can be under our feet also. Ask those bewildered sailors aboard the *Arizona*. Ask the Sullivan brothers and their additional brothers aboard the *Juneau* . . .

One morning, having chipped away with my hatchet for some time (my weapon and ice-cleaver was losing its edge, and I was too impatient to wield a file), I raised the block of ice to see frozen into it a small fish that I could not identify. I took the ice to the slab of concrete that served as an apron at the south entrance, and there I chipped until the fish fell free. I expected it to move its gills, expected it then to curl and to jump, as if hoping somehow to regain the channel. But though the fish looked beautifully preserved, it neither worked a gill nor made any effort whatsoever to find its lost current. The fish was dead.

In *The Immense Journey* Loren Eiseley's account of a similar entrapment has more of the miracle in it than does mine, though the miracle in his story does not finally save the fish. His was a catfish; he saw it encased in ice one morning as he was walking a tributary of the Platte. He blocked it out and dropped the block into a can. Several hours later, at home, he went down into the basement to check the ice and his fish, and lo! the fish's gills were laboring slowly in the icewater. "A thin stream of silver bubbles rose to the surface and popped," Eiseley wrote. "A fishy eye gazed up at me protestingly."

Then the miracle proceeded: the fish spoke, asking its captor and redeemer for a container larger than the can to swim in.

Amazed and wanting to oblige, the anthropologist filled a tank and dropped the catfish into its water, where, Eiseley says, it spent the winter.

One night in early spring, however, the fish jumped out of the tank, and Eiseley found it the next morning dead on the floor. "Maybe, in some little lost corner of his brain," Eiseley wrote, "he felt, far off, the pouring of the mountain waters through the sandy coverts of the Platte." Loren Eiseley felt an enormous kinship with that fish: "He had for me the kind of lost archaic glory that comes from the water brotherhood. We were both projections out of that timeless ferment and locked as well in some greater unity that lay incalculably beyond us. In many a fin and reptile foot I have seen myself passing by — some part of myself, that is, some part that lies unrealized in the momentary shape I inhabit."

I took my little dead fish in my hands and carried it back to the hole from which it had been arrested in ice. Before dropping it into the hole I raised and lowered it three times: *In the name of the Father, and of the Son, and . . .*

Item: the breaking up and the drifting away of the ice.

To know a river listen to it change from one braided mass into hundreds of separate floes, then watch as the sun returns the floes to water.

When the breaking up began, when I first heard it early on a Monday morning, I thought I was dreaming; even the distant words from KRVN in their own way corroborated what was happening: *I think I'm down to my last broken heart.* But it was the ice, not the heart, that was breaking, and it creaked and groaned and popped and crashed, and when I pushed away the curtains on the sliding glass doors I saw that either I or the river was in motion, and for several long moments I could not discern the unmoved from the moving.

I plugged in the coffee pot, slipped quickly into trousers and shirt, socks and boots, coat and gloves and cap and slid open the glass doors and went to the balcony's east wooden railing, where I stood memorizing the reborn flow of the river. Chunks of every size and formation were floating evenly and almost pristinely on the surface. And though the movement was slow, the word that comes immediately to mind is *relentless.* Yesterday the river seemed locked forever into stasis; now, only a few hours later, it was flowing as if it meant to flow until time itself was exhausted. Before many more days have passed I will see and hear the first wedge of geese heading north, an elongated skein honking like old Fords. And I will note some chickadees skittering about, too, then a few ducks—orange bills, black heads and backs, white sides and bellies. Other birds, too, will begin to assemble, including those small colorful ones that seem to enjoy walking on the undersides of limbs, as if Newton were yet to be invented. And the two bald eagles that have their nests atop the highest tree on the island between the cabin and the far shore—they will continue their watch, their high, slow-motion circling.

I pour myself a cup of hot black coffee and return to the railing. I cannot watch the movement of the floes closely enough, how the river like a snake of kaleidoscope changes as the floes jockey their snow-capped thoroughbred haunches for position, as minute by minute the reflections and shadows brighten and darken, darken and brighten with the rising of the sun. And, mind you, there is absolutely not so much as a split second of intermission. *Relentless.* Shut your eyes: the breaking up, the moving on, continues. Turn your back: the floes glide on, oblivious to your existence.

I brought to the cabin not only the works of Nebraska authors, but also a copy of the *Old Farmer's Almanac.* It tells me that by the end of the week a hunter's moon will highlight the night sky, meaning that if the night is without clouds I will have a special treat for my wife when she arrives to take me home for the weekend.

My preparations for the event are calculated and elaborate. I do not open the large can of Dinty Moore beef stew, for example, nor do I drink all of the beer. I clean out the fireplace. I sweep the floor. I check the supply of wood. Earlier that week I had nailed together a makeshift bookcase, unpainted one-by-sixes for shelves and cottonwood limbs for legs. Now, anticipating a party with my wife under a full hunter's moon watching the floes move down the river, I set my scattered books and magazines in order, using the jerry-built bookcase as the order's linchpin.

The other half of the festivities arrives shortly before dusk, carrying a large brown paper sack from which she extracts the following: two potatoes wrapped in foil; a cold six-pack of dark longneck beer; various chips and condiments; and two T-bone steaks, each as large as one of the larger floes. Before I can tell her of my plan—which includes the suggestion that we stay the night at the cabin—she has told me hers: Let's have a T-bone party, then stay the night at the cabin.

We do just that—and though my wife's plan, as I tell her, is probably the most innovative chunk of strategy since the advent of the ancient Babylonian orgy, I nonetheless make two contributions: the suggestion that we sit on the balcony and watch the river, and the slightly later suggestion that we switch from dark longneck beer to Chivas Royal Salute whiskey to aid in the watching.

A colleague (may God bless her) had given me a decorative bottle of Royal Salute, complete with a lavish purple pouch with a golden drawstring, and on my first day at the cabin I had placed it on a high shelf in the kitchen—then promptly had forgotten about it. Call it whatever you like—chance, divine intervention, the muse, the urge to contribute—but something that night as my wife and I sat on the balcony watching the placid relentless downriver movement of countless floes whispers *Royal Salute* into my starboard ear.

Deciphering the hint, I excuse myself and make my way downstairs to the kitchen. The lovely bottle in its purple pouch sits precisely where I had placed it, waiting. I reach down the bottle, open it, pour generous shots into two small jelly jars, to each add a dash of water, then holding both jars in one hand and the bottle in the other I return to the balcony.

I yodel softly to attract my wife's attention; she had been giving it all, as I knew she would, to the river. I hand her one of the jelly jars and by way of a toast I read from the bottle's label, depending upon the full hunter's moon for light:

> *By an ancient custom*
> *originating in the*
> *Royal Navy, a salute*
> *of twenty-one guns*
> *is the prerogative*
> *of the Reigning Sov-*
> *ereign. Royal Salute*
> *Whiskey, created to*
> *celebrate the coro-*
> *nation of Her Majesty,*
> *Queen Elizabeth,*
> *symbolizes this homage.*

We clink jars and indulge the first sip. We smack lips. "If it was good enough for Liz," I say, "it should be good enough for us."

After two more sips my wife wants to know where the ice is.

"In the river," I tell her. "Floating downstream."

"I mean for the whiskey," she says.

After several more sips she reverses her position. "Good whiskey," she says, having become an authority, "should be consumed at room temperature," *room* in this instance meaning *outdoors on a balcony watching a river.*

"And probably," I say, "good whiskey should not be contaminated with water."

"Ugh," says my wife, meaning that even good whiskey, without a dash of water, is an insult to the truly delicate palate.

Are we aboard a raft, my wife and I, under a full hunter's moon gliding with floes fore and aft, starboard and port, gliding relentlessly to John Neihardt's Missouri, to Mark Twain's Mississippi, to everyone's Caribbean? I believe that we are. Under us the planks of our raft dip and rise in the current; above us the same stars that teased and bewildered Huckleberry Finn tease and bewilder us. Jim, I believe you had it right: the moon—mother of all things night and everlasting—laid them. In a few weeks our younger daughter will look her fiancé in the eye and say *I do.* She wants a poem from me as the benediction. (Sweetheart, I say to my wife, would you like another Royal Salute?) With jars freshly filled I try these lines:

If you love me,
lie with me
here between the owl and river,
beneath the awful wheeling of a marriage moon.

Yes, *awful:* because it means here *awesome,* yet more than awesome—mix two parts awesome with one part thrilling apprehension and you have pretty much what I have in mind.

My wife is not listening. She is looking into her jelly jar, extrapolating, I believe, from its meager contents to the contents of the river. When I recite

Let the water in the river
be our home that can't stay home

she looks up and smiles. When I say

Let the earth, proud woman, old friend, roll over,
she smiles again.

Item: spending a full day beside and in the river with a four-year-old granddaughter.

Hike and whittle, I say, then back to the cabin for a glass of milk and a peanut-butter sandwich.

Michelle grins and nods. She turned four less than a month ago. Her hair is cornsilk, her eyes sky. She smiles easily, like Father Lightbody, but unlike those smiles from the priest hers every time seem to mean it. She wears white tennis shoes, yellow socks, yellow shorts, a green shirt — lime green, the color of the leaves on many of the saplings across the river. Her mother had left her on the south doorstep of the cabin, where I sat whittling, about ten o'clock; she would return for her, she said, sometime around dusk.

Sometime around dusk. The phrase is magic: *If there is magic on this planet, it is contained in dusk.* I would have eight hours to impress my granddaughter with my hermitage.

I select a walking stick for myself, none for Michelle; that will occur later. I check my right front pocket to make certain that I have two pocketknives, my well-honed Remington and the blunt-bladed Barlow. Shall we venture along the river?

This day in early April in the middle of the week is precisely the one you order from the Catalog of Consummate Days. A slight breeze coming from—who knows where? Who cares? Already the sun has cleared the east-shore bluffs and with its sharp slant is turning the rippled water into echelons of coins. And those lime-green leaves across the way: look at them, I dare you, without the mouth watering.

We hike upstream to observe some of the wonders of this my adopted universe. Or is it the other way around? Has this river, with its endless shoreline, adopted me? We talk. In one more year my granddaughter will enter a kindergarten room to begin an education that I pray never ends. She is full of talk—some of it the question, some of it the answer, some of it suspended in between.

I take her first to Woodpecker Haven, several huge dead upright cottonwoods with woodpecker holes enough to suggest at least a battalion. We watch the birds suddenly appear, just as suddenly disappear; when they seem to have been swallowed by the holes for good, they reappear, cock their heads at us as if we are trees too strange to be pecked at, then off they fly to sharpen the points of their beaks, perhaps, or to meet at a bath with their buddies to tip a drink or two and talk things over.

Off then to Logjam Ravine, where we sit facing each other on separate logs, it being high time, I say, to rest our bones. And to whittle.

I take the Barlow from my pocket, open its blade, hand the knife to Michelle. I had picked up a length of sumac shortly after leaving the cabin and had given it to my granddaughter, who accepted it as if it were in some peculiar fashion a finished product.

Carefully I show her how to press the thin edge of the blade against the bark of the sumac, how to move the blade then slowly downward, shaving away the bark. She is a bright young lady. She catches on quickly. Soon she is shaving away the bark like a trooper. At this rate her walking stick will be more or less finished at one sitting.

Her small delicate hands are the same hands that in several years will beat me at a game of jacks that I honestly believed I could win. I had not played jacks for the good part of half a century, but when Michelle tossed down the gauntlet I not only accepted the challenge, I believed I would triumph. I was, after all, much older; but even more important than age was the apprenticeship I had gone through with my sister. She had been the unofficial jacks champion of our hometown, and I could take day-to-day advantage of her expertise. Ones, twos, threes, fours. Eggs in the basket. Pigs in the pen.

We went outside to the front porch, which was a thick slab of uneven concrete, and the first premonition I had that I might not win came to me as I tried to sit cross-legged on the concrete. The body did not bend as readily as it had when I was under apprenticeship with my sister. I tried two or three times to force the joints into compliance, but each time they resisted—forcefully. Finally I had to settle for a position too awkward and much too uncomfortable to describe. Michelle—who had assumed the cross-legged position in one brief and liquid motion—was meanwhile watching my antics with something akin to bemused pity, as if for all practical purposes the match had already ended.

For all practical purposes it already had. She cleaned, in the country idiom, my plow. Ones, twos, threes, fours. Eggs in the basket. Pigs in the pen. And so on. But earlier I had further sensed my demise when I took my first turn; the rubber ball seemed to have grown smaller over the years, and my hands unaccountably larger, the knuckles on the fingers less inclined to take instruction. Then when Michelle took her first turn (she had graciously insisted that I lead off: age before beauty, my mother would have said), I could detect right away that the old plow was about to be scoured.

I had erred by believing what I had been taught to believe: anything truly mastered can be quickly and easily returned to. One month almost to the day before playing jacks with my granddaughter I had applied this idiotic adage to the riding of a bicycle—had retrieved my black three-speed Schwinn from the basement, had dusted it off and inflated the tires, had mounted it then for a ten-block voyage west on Huntington.

Early spring. All of the long winter's snow and ice had melted, leaving numerous potholes at irregular intervals along the street. And as I rode along, now pedaling, now coasting, weaving among the potholes as if in world-class slalom in slow motion, I remembered how as a boy delivering the *Wichita Beacon* I would sometimes see how far I could pedal without keeping my hands on the handlebars—and how sometimes I did this while riding on the sidewalk in front of my girlfriend's house. As I now remembered it, I had been a blue-chipper at riding my bicycle without hands; as I now remembered it, I had several times negotiated the entire route without once touching the handlebars. No doubt my girlfriend sooner or later had seen this; no doubt she had been impressed.

At 56th Street I managed a U-turn without stopping. I was

two blocks into the return trip when I decided to impress my girlfriend.

My girlfriend, as it happened, was an elderly woman standing in her front yard leaning on a rake. I had traveled at least one block with my hands free of the handlebars; very deftly, with subtle movements of the body, I had avoided every pothole. Encouraged, I had increased speed.

Huntington Street is not hilly; but it is not altogether flat, either. I believe that I was on the down side of a gradual slope, gaining speed, when I saw the elderly woman and she saw me. Now what goes through the mind of an elderly woman who looks up from her rake to see a grown man riding a black three-speed Schwinn toward her, his hands not touching the handlebars, his arms raised and extended as if in a benediction?

Whatever she might have been thinking, she waved. And I waved back—a sustained and vigorous wave, a wave behind which resided a face with a grin on it as wide almost, but not nearly as deep, as the pothole I hit point blank.

To this day I regret that I do not have this tragedy on film. I described a perfect 360-degree somersault, landing perfectly in the position I had started from; I rose to my feet, perfectly in control, perfectly unscathed. My black three-speed Schwinn lay in the gutter, its front wheel perfectly destroyed. I turned to the elderly woman to complete what—had the pothole not intervened—would surely have been the perfect wave, and the elderly woman perfectly shook her head. In the morning my body would ache—perfectly, *all the way from hell to breakfast.*

A month later that same body would be doing a flip-flop of a different kind: my granddaughter flaying it unmercifully at jacks.

Yet here is my consolation: I was losing at jacks—at a game that, like bicycling, cannot be quickly or easily returned to—but I was winning at Watching My Granddaughter Savoring Victory. It is a skill that she too might one day master; it is a game that only the loser can win.

I have taken my Remington from my pocket and am whittling for its own olfactory and tactile sake as I watch my granddaughter cut away the last of the sumac's bark. She has worked at it tenaciously and steadily, biting her lower lip with the effort. When the last sliver falls to the ground she sighs deeply, then with the knife in hand runs her fingers over the wood, as if searching for some trace of bark she might have overlooked. She finds none. She knows what we both know: the stick is perfect.

Before returning to the cabin for milk and a peanut butter sandwich we explore a small portion of a bur oak opening, an expanse of fully matured bur oaks that in a dozen years will be the major part of the state's most scenic and ambitious parks. Michelle with her sumac walking stick asks questions that frequently I must resort to improvisation to answer. How old is this bur oak? How old is this one? Where did this bur oak come from? (Older than your mother's mother, sweetheart, older than your grandfather's father. I reckon the moon laid them.) When I tell her to look at the trees through squinted eyes she says how much they look like human beings.

Yes, I say, and just feel how thick their skin is, and she selects a tree whose giant branches like the arms of the saguaro curve upward at the elbows. With her small white fingers she touches the thick crust of the bur oak's bark—thick and corky, extending to cover even the smallest branches. Because of this thick bark, I tell her, the bur oak was the only tree capable of surviving a prairie fire.

What is *surviving*? What is a *prairie fire*? Who in this bowling alley bowled the sun?

When we return to the cabin we return on legs related to rubber. The milk, kept cold with a block of ice hatcheted from the river, has the flavor of nectar. And the peanut butter sandwich? Finished with one, we have another.

Then Michelle—this lovely little engine of energy—surprises me: she wants a nap. She surprises me further: she wants to sleep outside, on a pallet in the shade of the locust, not more than a dozen paces from the river.

As she sleeps I try not to; I am on a deck chair, reading Mari Sandoz, taking a breather now and then to break, as if the ultimate code, the mystery of the water.

Now here is a curious thing: my granddaughter opens her eyes from sleep as I am finishing a Pawnee version of creation.

It seems that many of the earth's creatures were asleep for untold ages in a vast dark cave. One day one of the creatures, Buffalo Woman, opens her eyes, rubs them, looks searchingly in each of the four great directions, seeing only in the last one a pinpoint of light. Carefully then, and slowly, she moves about the cave, waking one creature, then another, until the entire assemblage is at last awake, rubbing their eyes, waiting for her to guide them.

And she does. In single file they follow her as she makes her way in deliberate and measured steps toward the pinpoint of light. Little by little the pinpoint grows larger, the heartbeat of each creature meanwhile growing louder, growing stronger. At last they arrive at the source of the light—an arched doorway leading onto a wide distended ledge overlooking the essentials of Eden: much grass, many buffalo, a wide stream filled to its banks with running water. The ledge is Pahuk Point; the stream—the Platte River. I watch Michelle come awake. Her pallet had been a sleeping bag atop one blanket and a comforter. From the bag she emerges as if from a soft cocoon, rubbing her eyes, and for a moment I see her as the Pawnee woman about to lead her people from darkness into light, from the poverty of death into the richness of life.

And, in a sense, Michelle does just that, because for the rest of the day, until *sometime around dusk,* she busies herself with the rock and the river, assembling and dissembling, gathering and yielding, collecting and giving away.

Here is the pattern: she looks for small rocks, rocks that in size and shape and color and texture measure up to her inexplicable criteria. She makes a small mound of these rocks, a cairn, and when the mound satisfies, she throws the rocks slowly, one by one, into the river. This done, she waits the rough duration of several sips of Country Time lemonade, then standing demurely at my side poses the question: Do you think we can find them?

Why not?

We kick off our shoes and pull off our socks (I am wearing a swimming suit in the guise of denim shorts) and walk hand in hand into the river. From one current to another we move, the water seldom more than ankle-deep (though there are sudden surprising exceptions), Michelle stopping from time to time to bring up a twig, a weed, a handful of sand. When occasionally her stooping brings forth a small rock she studies it long and hard to determine if it is in fact one of those that she had thrown—one she had gathered and stacked and designated as family—or an outsider wanting to weasel its way in. With unlimited awe I watch her: this one she'll keep (she gives it to me to hold in my left hand or to put into my pocket), this one goes back into the water. Well, I think, this business of playing God takes more insight than I'll ever live to achieve, and more confidence; and so it is that I serve merely as sidekick as we splash from current to current, sandbar to sandbar, gathering back the bones.

Until Michelle says, That's it, her determination no doubt influenced by this fact: neither of our free hands, nor any of my pockets, can hold another rock.

Back on shore, Michelle arranges the rocks on a blue towel draped over the barkless stump of a cottonwood. As the rocks dry she gives each a name, in her mind's eye dresses them and gives them their freedom. Thus in their own static way they move about, in their own heavy way experience pain and pleasure. But chiefly they grow old quickly, and when Michelle sees that they have lived long enough she gathers them into a mound and one by one—each with a thrust worthy of omnipotence—she returns them back to the ongoing lotus of the river. When the last one strikes the water she begins again her search for the first rock to use to assemble another mound . . .

Sometime around dusk. When my granddaughter's mother returns it is precisely *sometime around dusk.* Because the cabin sits low in this valley on the sunset side of the river, dusk arrives early. But you can look across the river to the other shore and for the longest time see sunshine, can watch as the brilliant lime on the leaves of the saplings activates saliva at both sides of the tongue.

Michelle with her perfect sumac walking stick slides into the front seat of the car beside her mother. She is four. Her hair is cornsilk, her eyes sky. When she smiles, and she smiles often, I believe she means it.

If you watch the far side of the river long enough, it too turns to dusk, then to deep shadow, then to the darkness you already are in—and have been in for almost an hour. If you go to the balcony to await the rising of a full marriage moon, you can trust this adage: It will happen. Because it has happened countless times before, it will happen again.

For it is the source
Of Afton that I seek and dread,
Compelled to marvel at movement and
To worship visible fountainheads.
—"The Spring House"

To know a river, float it in a 12-foot johnboat every summer for thirty summers. Try the Platte, and enjoy it—the braided currents, the expansive shores, the innumerable sandbars and islands. As you half recline in the boat, resting the oars, think of all those westward-ho pioneers whose souls reached this river to follow it—wherever. Of those who made it and of those who didn't. Of locust. Typhoid. Bottlejaw. Kangaroo rat. Grasshopper. Cholera. Smallpox. Tick. Blizzard. Colic. Distemper. Think of this river as a haven for the crane, the eagle, the goose, the tern, the plover. Think of what one of the pioneers, James Evans, said of the Platte in his *Journal of a Trip to California:*

My first impression on beholding the Platte River was, that as it looked so wide and so muddy, and rolled along within three feet of the top of the bank with such majesty that it was unusually swollen and perfectly impassable. Judge my surprise when I learned that it was only three or four feet deep. . . . The water is exceedingly muddy, or I should say sandy; and what adds greatly to the singular appearance of this river, the water is so completely filled with glittering particles of micah or isinglass that its shining waves look to be rich with floating gold.

Think of the Platte. Then, summer in and summer out, float the Loup.

Because of this: the Loup is a homegrown Nebraska river, its central and northern branches beginning in the Sandhills of Cherry County, its southern branch with its fountainhead not far from Stapleton in Logan County. And just as the Loup knows where to begin, it knows where to end: just below Columbus.

Spring, meaning a flow, a fountainhead, is a mystery I do not care to have explained. Heacock's Reservoir began with a fountainhead enshrined within a stone house, the clear cold water rising and rising into a trough that carried it from the house to drop it into a shallow gulley that carried it over red earth and through a grove of catalpas to the reservoir, so that by the time it reached the pool it was sufficiently roiled and muddied to suit the tastes of the carp and the catfish and the turtles. I loved to fish in that reservoir, to sneak away from home with a cane pole and a dozen obese nightcrawlers in a Prince Albert can, to hop a slow freight train if one happened along; but at times I chose to take an alternate route, to walk west beside the blacktop so that I might drink from Heacock's spring before moving on down to the reservoir.

On a stifling day — mid-July, maybe, maybe early August — you could hardly wait to reach the spring house. By the time you entered its side door you would have been drenched, sweat coursing the stomach and the spine in a sweltering aggravation of rivulets. You would place cane pole and can on the floor, then moving to the corner of the house where a large rectangle of concrete enclosed the spring, forming a basin, you would lie on your stomach to drink the cold clear rising water—to drink, and to press an open eye all the way to the gravel-scoured bottom of clarity.

On certain extra-hot occasions I drank that cold and immaculate water until I swear I became the heavy-bellied catfish I had come for. I remember how difficult it was on those occasions to disengage my fins and force myself to my bulky clumsy landlocked feet. I would stand immobile for several seconds, blinking, then walk half-drunkenly in a circle, trying to find my legs. When my vision had cleared, and the legs were steady, I would pick up the cane pole and the can of worms and hike appreciatively, as if with eyes reborn, down to the reservoir.

The sources of the North and the Middle Loups must be the big brothers to the source of Heacock's Reservoir. Covering an area of more than 19,000 square miles, the Nebraska Sandhills make up one of the largest sand dune areas in the Western Hemisphere. They measure, east to west, about 265 miles; south to north, at the widest point, 130 miles. Some say its shape resembles an egg; others say a diamond. I opt for both: eggs for its fragility—eggshell and topsoil vegetation not much thicker than a shim—diamond for its priceless and hardheaded inclination to stick around.

To appreciate both sides of this apparent contradiction drive with me to the northwest quarter of the state. After a cheeseburger and a beer at the corner hotel in Hyannis, we will take Highway 2 west to Ellsworth, where we say we are stopping for gas, but where in fact we use the fillup as an excuse to buy something made of leather put together by a craftsman who supports his talents through the sale of gas and oil. From Ellsworth we head due north on Highway 27. Twenty miles later we will turn east to follow a couple of backroads that will take us to the grave of Mari Sandoz.

The lone grave is on the side of a sandhill overlooking Old Jules' transplanted orchard—apple and peach and plum trees in long thick lines of open defiance, Old Jules himself having defied almost everything, weather and terrain and hearsay and his several wives included, to get the trees planted and watered. The grave is protected from the Hereford and the Angus by several tiers of barbed wire; you enter the protected arena through a small-slatted gate rigged with a pulley and a sashweight. Inside, you walk uphill to the large granite tombstone and, standing behind it, you behold the Sandhills.

Or you *would* behold them, if you had eyes equipped to see forever. Beyond the myriad dunes and hogbacks immediately before you, dunes kept pretty much intact with needlegrass and switchgrass, dropseed and bluestem, soapweed and grama, spiderwort, thistle, primrose, sand cherry, ivy, and redroot, flow the Snake and the Niobrara Rivers, along and between them a scattering of red cedar, pine, box elder, hackberry, cottonwood, wild plum, chokecherry, and elm.

Say that the month is March. Say that at the moment you do not need a sweater, though you brought one with you.

If your eyes are impossibly keen they might be seeing far away to the east the largest county in the Sandhills, the largest in all of Nebraska—Cherry. On one of the ranches—a modest though somewhat comfortable one, say 4,500 acres—a rancher with his hired hand is caking the cattle, after which they will ear-tag several of the youngsters, during which time they will undergo half a dozen interruptions to help a cow or a heifer with her calving. Now look closely. See that Angus heifer? She's in trouble; they'll have to use the calf puller. They affix the puller's clamp to the protruding hooves to winch the wet black blob to birth. Notice how the mother in agony dropped at the last moment to her knees, then fell on her right side. Notice how quickly, though, following the birth, she is back on her feet, how soon thereafter she is circling her calf—curious, bewildered—afterbirth trailing her like a slick bloody rope. And what is the hired hand doing? He is sprinkling the supine calf with what you'd hear him call "Calf Coaxer" if he weren't a hundred leagues away. Does it work? Yes—its blood aroma attracts the heifer, and she begins to lick.

That large space nearest the barn, the one teeming with cows and heifers whose bags appear tight to the point of bursting—that's the heavy lot; it is filled with those animals the rancher and his hired hand believe are closest to coming light. That one just there, for example—can you see her? She had dropped not only her calf but also her calf bed, a goodly portion of her innards. Now watch the rancher and his sidekick. They will place the dangling pear-shaped innards into a five-gallon can; the hired man will hold this can while the rancher works the innards back into the wall-eyed cow. Eventually, if all goes well, all of the entrails inch by gut-slick inch will be returned, and the rancher will sew the ruptured skin together, wash his hands at the pump, and be ready for another.

But note that most of the calves arrive without incident, several hundred on this ranch alone before the end of March. Watch them watch their mothers licking them clean. Watch them struggle to find their legs, how with the help of the mother each noses its way to where already the milk from its bursting udder is dripping. You ever have the feeling that whatever isn't round wants to be?

Sure, says the hired hand (after supper, after roast beef and mashed potatoes and iced tea and macaroni and two types of cheeses with hot rolls and cherry Jell-O and a wedge of chocolate cake under an impressive dollop of vanilla ice cream with hot black coffee to wash it down—and when there is a lull out in the heavy lot), I'll answer a question or two, if I can.

Yep, most female bovines do have their little eccentricities, especially when they are about to give birth. For one thing, they prefer at least a handful of privacy. The cow by and large prefers hers at the top of a hill, but the heifer will take her privacy wherever it happens, ridgetop or otherwise. The heifer's offspring will ordinarily weigh around forty-five to fifty pounds, the cow's around fifty to sixty-five pounds. But exceptions—how do you say it?—*abound,* and one reason is that sometimes a heifer will be bred to a type of bull whose get produces large calves. The Galvey bull is one of those, and the Saler bull—that's a French breed with balls so prolific they rhyme with *beaucoup.*

Absolutely: The windmill had been a big part of the Sandhills since long before Hector was a pup, and I don't see it drying up in the near future. That one north of the house pumps water not only for the cattle, but also sends water down the slope to the pasture. We have five windmills on this spread, and all of them pump water.

Your ranch horse, if it's worth its feed, should be ambidextrous, part cutting horse, part roping horse—and it should be a horse willing to take its rider to either of two places: nowhere or anywhere. My own horse, Rowdy, used to be but isn't now; I tamed him with an axhandle.

Barbed wire? Some say barb wire, some bobwore. I spent a couple of lifetimes one summer in Texas, so you prob'ly know which one I prefer. Mostly around here you'll see red-strand bobwore. That's because the barbs are painted red—or were, when the wore was new. The barbs are double and are spaced about one dick length apart, give or take. This morning I saw a new calf attack two strands of that wore, and the wore won.

No, the Sandhills coyote is not extinct, and prob'ly never will be. Saw one a couple of days ago, but couldn't get off a shot. A good pelt during a good season will bring seventy-five or eighty dollars. Last year, though, the average was about fifty dollars. Nope, I don't skin them; I hang them up and keep them as cold as the weather permits until a fur trader takes them off my hands. Yes, there are indeed quite a few traders come through here. You'd be surprised. And even with the high cost of ammunition—six bucks for twenty shells—you can make money, if you can hit what you're aiming at.

Well, the blowout happens when the vegetation here, such as it is, gets overgrazed or trampled down, leaving the sand at the mercy of the wind. Ranchers don't care to see this happen; on occasion I have heard my own dear boss mutter improprieties when he comes across a fresh blowout. He doesn't even approve of the cattle socializing in clusters at the windmills, after they've had their fill of water. The more the cattle go to clustering in the same spot, the more likely that spot will become a blowout. It takes a long time, years most generally, for a blowout to recover its lost vegetation. Sand: it's what a lot of folks fly to to lie on to have something to call *vacation*. Here, sand is what you don't want to see unless most of it is being held in place with grasses. I need another cup of coffee. How about you?

You remain at the grave of Mari Sandoz, just off Highway 27 northwest of Hyannis and straight down from Gordon, to watch the dunes slowly darken into an eerie and mysterious void as the sun sets behind you. Sure enough, the Sandhills coyote is not extinct. If it is, how can you hear one howling? And the deer and the bobcat, the porcupine and the occasional red fox—out there in the void somewhere they sniff and lay their plans. They move and persist.

Move and persist. Under your feet as you leave the gravesite you can feel movement, the weight of your brief biped existence making itself known against 19,000 square miles of ancient and distinctive and bullheaded sponge. Sand, yes; hills, yes. Simple addition: sand + hills equals Sandhills.

No. The Sandhills are more than the sum of their parts. Because above the sand grow grasses sufficient to sustain some of the largest cattle ranches in the country, if not the world. Because, wounded by blowouts, the prairie penstemon and other tenacious members of the figwort family come eventually to their rescue. Because in its own diverse and resourceful ways the loose earth collects and stores its rainwater, permits it to flow horizontally to the swales and flats to become, say, one of the seventeen lakes in Cherry County, lakes with nothing short of magic in their names: Shell, Pelican, Rat, Mother, Swan, Red Deer, Willow, Dads, Cottonwood, Beaver. Because these lakes, and countless others like them, are tangible liquid evidence of what lies below—the High Plains aquifer, the Ogallala aquifer, 174,000 square miles of phenomenon that stretch from Texas to South Dakota, enough water to fill if not overflow Lake Huron.

And because it is the spring from which the North and Middle Loups begin.

To know a river, decide which river you want most to know. Then push your boat into the nearest current.

I did this for the first time thirty years ago. I did not own a boat thirty years ago—and I have otherwise well-intentioned colleagues who might venture that I do not own one yet— my vessel being a 12-foot aluminum johnboat, Appleby by trade name. My argument is this: if it floats and gets you there, it is a boat. Their argument is—never mind. Their argument is nothing more than a canoe with holes in it, all of them on the lower deck.

My maiden voyage, as it turned out, skirted disaster. I had put my trust in an acquaintance who did in fact own a boat, a thick-gauged wide-hulled iron-masted abberation he had christened, appropriately, *Diamond-in-the-Rough,* and appropriately had sacrificed a longneck bottle of Lone Star for the christening. My acquaintance said that he knew how to read a river, most especially the Loup, because he had gone to the State Historical Society and it had plied him with relief maps detailing the Loup River all the way from—hell to breakfast. I believed him. So did my brother, whose leg to this day carries the scar of the spurting artery. So did my brother's friend who, like me and Maclean and Eiseley and probably untold others, has a fear of water he loves not to resist.

We covered the dining-room table with maps until they spilled onto the floor; then we covered the floor. We penciled and planned far into the night; neither tactical nor strategic fine points were left uncovered. On our knees, beer in one hand and a hi-lighter in the other, we described a river route calculated to quench that thirst for adventure that the Falstaff could not touch. Finally, this question: Should we load the boat tonight?

By all means—or by any. Atop my Bel-Air Chevrolet, the one that one day would take me to St. Patrick's Church to discuss the efficacy of baptism with Father Lightbody, we loaded my acquaintance's *Diamond-in-the-Rough,* one of us remembering, at the last moment, the oars.

That night a rain so gentle it scarcely interrupted my sleep—I was adrift on a mattress, reading the channel with impeccable foresight—fell, but by morning the clouds had floated far to the west and a brilliant August sunrise portended nothing but the dry warm smell of success. Having noted the sunrise through the living-room window, I stepped outside to admire the Bel-Air with its boat, both poised streetward in the driveway as if for flight. I saw right away that we had not loaded the boat properly; we had placed her upright, intending to use her glandular space for the loading of gear. Into that space, or into much of it, the rain had fallen, enough rain to cause the ivory portion of my tan-under-ivory vehicle to collapse. The scene registered itself heavily upon the mammalian section of my brain. Christ, I remember thinking, what have we done?

I passed the word to my comrades; soon we were taking turns on the ladder, using a two-pound Folgers coffee can as a bailer. Last night, in our planning, we had not thought to include a bailer as part of the gear; now, bailing, I suggested that we take one—this very one, in fact, since it seemed to be doing its work efficiently enough, albeit slowly.

The boat at last free of water we untied and lowered her onto the lawn; then moving as if a well-trained unit we deployed ourselves deliberately and precisely inside the Bel-Air, my brother and I in the back seat, my acquaintance and my brother's friend in the front seat, and on the count of three we pressed our collective palms upward until the top of my lovely Chevrolet exploded like an M-80 back to its predeflated configuration.

This time we loaded the *Diamond* upside-down, securing her with perhaps more rope and bungee cords than necessary. Into the trunk we forced our gear.

We did not take much gear because we had planned only a two-night float, and because August in Nebraska rarely calls for coats. And because I had promised plenty of catfish for the evening meals, we did not have to pack much food—an egg or two for breakfast, with some bacon and a couple of hotcakes, sardines and baloney and cheese sandwiches for lunch. And a bottle of something less than Royal Salute with a couple of beers to settle things down.

The drive from Lincoln to the Fullerton Bridge, where we would put the *Diamond* onto the river, was one hundred miles of sunlight and anticipation, of dawdling and of speeding up and of stopping—at Central City, for example, where we found a hardware store almost without parallel: yes, they did have tent stakes in stock, and, yes, they did sell them separately from the tents. We bought a dozen because my brother's friend, who was furnishing the tent, had forgotten the stakes, but luckily for all of us, he said, he remembered that he had forgotten them, and he did the remembering in time for all of us to chip in and buy four more stakes than we needed, just in case.

The shank of the day was pretty much history when after a snack in Fullerton, just to tide us over, we pushed the *Diamond* into the clean clear sand-scoured water of the Loup River. Four pioneer spirits in a single boat adrift on a current two-thirds of which, at least, had begun as seepings in the Sandhills of Cherry County, the north branch with its birth not far from Piester Lake, the middle branch beginning its inexorable flow about twenty miles north of Hyannis—the other one-third, the south branch, oozing into the act ten miles west of Stapleton, near the line that divides McPherson and Logan Counties. O sweet Jesus! I know we are moving because the Fullerton Bridge, with its museum of artwork and graffiti, is slowly receding. This river, I tell myself, is the ultimate and the wisest compromise: it is not Shannon's Creek, from which my friend Oscar emerged grinning and gasping and sanctified, nor is it the Mississippi, Twain's lovely but sometimes ominous chameleon. It is instead a mid-sized river, its currents swift and plentiful enough to change from year to year the contours of some of the shoreline, yet not large enough to attract anything more exotic than an occasional airboat or a brace of youngsters with something more than wading on their minds.

Time is the stream we go a-floating in; almost before we know it the sun has taken on a tint of orange, and the owner of the boat, who has been doing the rowing and who has given all of us permission to call him either Captain or Skipper, allows that we should keep our eyes peeled for a good place to camp. This we do—because our Captain, after all, is our Captain, a man who knows the river because he had gone to the State Historical Society and it had given him a ton of relief maps detailing the Loup River all the way from hell to breakfast. These maps our Captain brought with him; he had bound them with brown twine into a bundle the size and heft of a Sears catalog, and he had stuffed them into a space at the back of the boat between the port side and the beer chest.

Our Captain is a rotund fellow who is perpetually good humored—until something goes wrong. At such a time his mood varies from slightly petulant to surly to downright unpleasant. At the moment, his chubby hands at the oars, he is happy; he has a round boyish face, its roseate cheeks, like the rest of him, a tad overweight, his brown hair going off in several directions. He sits with his back to the bow. He looks at me, grins, tells me to read the channel, then to pass my reading along to him: Heavy on the right oar, Skipper, for example, or hard on the left, Captain, or easy on both oars—I think we're smack in the middle of the channel and can let her float without much rowing.

When I misread the channel I hear for the first time a sound that is difficult to forget, a soft scraping of sand against the underside of the *Diamond,* a scraping that intensifies until our craft comes to a complete stop, the shallow water of the Loup moving on as if our hang-up doesn't matter. And it doesn't, not really; its irritation is so slight, in fact, that the Captain finds it more amusing than aggravating. He invites us to step out of the boat and push it back into the channel. We do—for he is our Captain, after all, a man who knows the river because . . .

After several further misreadings I and my fellow noncommissioned swab-jockeys find it difficult to smile while pushing the *Diamond* back into the channel. For one thing, the *Diamond-in-the-Rough* is a heavy and cumbersome boat, even when empty; loaded with gear—the chest of beer aft, our duffel bags and the tent with its new sack of tent stakes fore, not to mention our Captain sitting portly and ruddy amidships, shouting orders—the *Diamond* is a leviathan that might well have swallowed an anvil or two instead of Jonah. And another thing: there really isn't much of a channel to read, a bald fact that our Captain seems unable to assimilate. He sits there on a bench of thick-gauged aluminum, his hands on the oars, the business ends of the oars poised above the water as if at any moment the boat either on its own or at the behest of three barefooted yeomen might discover the channel, whereupon the oars will come to life to guide and encourage the *Diamond* downstream.

But the sad truth is that there isn't much of a channel to be discovered—not by the boat on its own, not by the three yeomen who pull and push until they have only enough strength left to threaten mutiny.

Our Captain removes his red tennis shoes and rolls up his pantlegs; he is wearing blue overalls and no shirt, meaning that his sunburn at the end of the voyage should be more decorative than any of ours, because we are wearing jeans and washpants and T-shirts—and one of us has a ball cap to protect the skull, another a wide-brimmed straw hat, while my brother protects his cranium with a sailor's cap loaned him by my Aquarian wife, who came by the cap by way of her older brother, who after the Japanese surrendered aboard the *Missouri* served long and honorably in the Seabees.

Our Captain takes the lead rope, worries a peculiar slip-knot into the loose end and manages somehow to force the noose down over his shoulders and chest so that, leaning his body, his midriff, against the noose he can bring an impressive amount of weight to bear in an effort to offset the *Diamond*'s considerable drag. By this time we yeomen have caught our breath and are fully prepared to do our share of the hauling and heaving.

When we find the trickle of a channel near the shore our vote is unanimous: this would indeed be an ideal spot to camp for the night. And, in fact, the spot if not ideal doesn't miss it by much. The bank is steep and a bit too high to be easily negotiated, but the area is fertile with dry wood for a campfire, and several cottonwoods, high as skyscrapers, should give us plenty of protection from the sunrays the following morning.

So is it my fault that I do not catch enough catfish for supper that evening? Is it my fault that I do not catch *any* catfish? The water on this side of the river is much too shallow for any fish larger than a minnow, and my legs are much too spent to go splashing across to explore the other side. The Loup is not as wide as the Platte (the latter having been translated by the Indians as *flat*, from the French), except occasionally, but after all its branches have come together it cannot by any means be characterized as narrow. Thus do I suggest cheese and baloney sandwiches—with at least one can of sardines, a few crackers, and a beer. We can worry about the last day's lunch when the last day comes.

My brother's friend (mine also, alias Leon) supervises the setting up of his tent, shows us where and how to hammer home each of the new tent stakes. The tent is old—heavy brown canvas that, erected, forms an elongated A though not quite elongated enough to accommodate comfortably four pioneer spirits, one of whom, our Captain, requires the better part of an acre, and two others, my brother and I, who aren't all that far behind. The fourth, alias Leon, though a virtual string-bean, nonetheless deserves something more than a strip no wider than a band-aid to lay his stringbean on.

But, as our Captain says (he has eaten, without outside intervention, two sandwiches and a can of sardines and a half box of crackers and has drunk a six-pack of Lone Star beer), who the hell cares? Is this a river voyage, he asks, or a panty raid? Are we mice or men? Bill, he says, would you toss me another beer?

Night descends. It is a warm night, and humid, but there is a breeze just strong enough to discourage mosquitoes. My brother had started a fire shortly after the securing of the final tent stake; perhaps he believed that I would find a way to catch a mess of catfish, or maybe he simply wanted to amuse himself with flames and coals. And soon enough the embers burn orange to blue to orange, and during a lapse in our campfire conversation I look up from staring at these embers to see a long low fork of lightning upstream. I tell our Captain.

But already he is in the tent, in his sleeping bag, his snoring as if a mating call to summon thunder. And how it works! Suddenly the breeze becomes a cool raging wind, flapping the tent, bending the cottonwoods. Just as suddenly the lightning is upon us, with its attendant thunder. And when the rain falls it falls both thick and horizontal.

Inside the tent, half soaked, we settle into our sleeping bags to lie out the storm. Fortunately, says the owner of the tent, I remembered that I forgot the tent stakes. Because now, he says (something philosophical in the way he says it), we have four extras.

Soon we are making use of them, driving them deep into soil that thanks to a layer of green sod affords a minimal purchase. We are not long at doing this, at driving the stakes and affixing four ropes from the stakes to grommets at the sides of the tent, but when we return to our sleeping bags we have been thoroughly immersed: in the name of the Father, and of the Son . . .

Our Captain meanwhile snores on. He has twisted himself and his sleeping bag so that now he is lying at an odd angle, usurping some of his crewmen's space. I sit on the dampening floor of the tent and with both feet push at the lower half of our Skipper's body, hoping to reduce the angle. Surprisingly, I succeed; the mass inside the sleeping bag both slides and snorts, and when it has been returned to a right angle I desist.

With my fellow Aquarians I do what I can to dry myself. In addition to four pioneer spirits, the tent shelters four duffel bags; we dip into three of them to bring forth a towel here, a dry pair of trousers there, a shirt that is only damp over yonder. The search for something waterless is not easy. No one had remembered to bring a flashlight. Fortunately, as Leon says, sotto voce, we have the incessant lightning to guide us. Another problem is that the wind is whipping the ancient tent so forcefully, and in gusts so menacingly violent, that it drives the rain through the brown canvas, refining it in the process so that it thickens the inside of the tent with a mist like a heavy fog.

Even so, we persist. Perhaps in our ears yet rings the rhetorical encouragement of our Captain: Is this a river voyage or a panty raid? Are we mice or men?

We lie without speaking, half dry, half damp, the other ten percent merely drenched. The wind and the rain slap at the tent, whipping and abusing and contorting it, until I begin to wonder whether we might not finally lose the tent to the storm, and all of us with it. I could imagine the water rising and rising until in a rush of indescribable power it would burst over the bank and carry away in a mad frothy swirling downward rush everything in its path. I had heard of rivers doing this, and had seen pictures. And now I see a picture with all four of us in it, four faces with four sets of open eyes staring quizzically into the eye of the camera they will never see.

As if to punctuate my half-dream lightning strikes; the sound is that of an M-80 firecracker, say, exploded half an inch away from the eardrum. I can hear then the futile resistance of the cottonwood—a creak gives way to a groan that rises steadily in pitch and increases steadily in volume until— how many eons later?—a thousand twigs and limbs crash brokenly against and into the waterlogged ground.

I hear myself saying, Missed us.

I hear my brother saying, This must be the end of the world.

I hear Leon saying, Lucky I remembered I forgot those tent stakes.

I hear our undaunted Captain, snoring on.

When the storm ends it ends so suddenly none of those not sleeping can believe it. For a long time we lie in silence, waiting for that inevitable sortie. But it doesn't happen. I do not want to interrupt this beautiful calm, do not want to chance anything that might break this wind-free, rain-free spell. So when I move to disengage the tent flaps to look outside, I do it quietly. In the far distance I see a remnant of lightning now and then disclose a billowing of sky. When I look up I see nothing but stars.

Now we lie in our sleeping bags as if creatures suddenly disgorged from a sea that has held us and nurtured us and shaped us for at least a million years. We find first our legs, each in turn moving silently outside to view however dimly the devastation, then we find our tongues. I feel like I'm Jonah, Leon says, though he adds that he doesn't know how Jonah, himself disgorged, felt. We talk about Jonah, then about Noah, and when I say that the lightning striking the cottonwood sounded like an enormous firecracker I think of Carter Leroy Hays.

A year before saving my brother at Ely's Sandpit, Carter taught me how to hold a Black Cat firecracker until the final instant, how to flick it then in front of me to watch it explode not more than twelve inches from the fingers. I was practicing this sleight-of-hand one late morning behind the outhouse, the same facility destined before long to burn to the ground. For some inexplicable reason I lit a cracker without having adequately noted the length of its fuse. (Length of fuse is critical, Carter had told me, and each cracker, he said, has its own individual fuse.) I stood watching the fuse burn, holding it closer to the face than Carter had advised, when pssssst! the fuse was gone, the cracker exploded, and I stood dumbfounded and disbelieving, the skin on my left palm split all the way from lifeline to thumb, my face burning, my nose thick with the acrid stench of potassium nitrate.

I went directly to the house and into the kitchen, where Mother stood at the wood range stirring something. I expected, at the least, pity; I hoped for, at the most—if she deemed it necessary—some form of last rite. Yes, Mother, I have sinned: I failed to predict accurately the burning fuse-life of a Black Cat firecracker. Probably I will die soon. Even so, Mother, attempt to heal me; that failing, Mother, forgive me.

What it was Mother was stirring must have needed the bulk of her attention. She looked at me, said nothing, returned to the stirring; when she paused again she did it to lift the spoon to note the thickness of whatever it was she was stirring. I believe that it was roast beef gravy, its recipe no doubt from my German grandmother. Something dark and thick and steaming oozed like a miniature waterfall down from the tip of the silver spoon. For several long moments Mother watched the gravy ooze from the spoon to fall in slow motion back into a deep black skillet, my own moment of judgment likewise in the hand of my mother and drawing nearer and nearer. Mother, I have sinned: I failed to predict accurately . . .

I am surely not more than a few paces from the doorstep of death. I look down at my left palm; the split in the skin is a red river, flowing. I inhale deeply. The nose is a cache of powder, burning.

My mother cleans the spoon with an index finger, raises the finger to her mouth to taste the gravy. She smacks her lips. She nods.

When she turns to me I stand straight as a soldier, straight as the onward Christian soldier must have stood before he marched onward. I am that soldier. I do not want to die, but in my heart I try to believe that I am ready.

Mother looks me up and down. She smacks her lips. She nods. Well, she says at last, I hope you're satisfied.

But the flood I want to tell you about, I say (we are talking louder now, and with more confidence; the storm seems not to be returning), happened the evening Carter introduced me to the M-80. I have something to show you, he said, motioning for me to follow him. It's a secret weapon.

Without saying anything he walked all the way to the back door of the Baptist church, I as if a good collie close at his heels. When he reached the back door, he turned and said, quietly this time, Follow me.

The back door was not locked. In my hometown the Baptists did not believe in dances, drinking, swearing, makeup, whoring, lasciviousness, irony, or the locking of the church's back door.

I followed my teacher through the door and down a flight of steps that led to the basement—a large square room, its concrete unadorned with the worldliness of either paint or wallpaper, its half-dozen concrete pillars giving it the appearance of an underground refuge at once mysterious and permanent. It smelled like my German grandmother's cave. Do you know how that ditty goes, "The wise man built his house upon the rock"? The basement of the Baptist church reminded me of that song, and at the time I was young enough not to question or to marvel at the irony of a Baptist being wise.

Carter had turned on a couple of lights. Don't worry, he said, the curtains on all the windows are closed.

He led me to the women's bathroom. We entered. He switched on the light.

Here, he said, is the secret weapon.

From a pocket he pulled an M-80, the first I had ever seen. He handed it to me. It's a firecracker, Carter explained. It blows hell out of anything.

I believed him. The cracker was round and red, easily as large as my little brother's metronomic pecker that day he galloped into the water at Ely's Sandpit.

And look, said Carter, at the fuse!

He explained that the casing of the fuse was waterproof, that we could light the fuse, drop the cracker into the stool there in the women's room in the basement of the Baptist church, and because the fuse was impervious to liquids it would stay ignited and the cracker would explode.

Carter had one nagging, one overwhelming, question: What sound would the cracker make should its large tube of powder explode somewhere in the dark and distant bowels of the church's plumbing?

To find out, Carter said, we must light the fuse, drop the cracker into the bowl, flush, then stand aside quietly with both ears open.

I watched my mentor as with nimble fingers he struck a match and put the flame to the tip of the fuse. At once a hissing, as if that first snake in Eden, sounded, and tiny sparks shot forth in a tiny shower from the casing. Carter did not hold this one as he did the Black Cat until the final instant; instead, he dropped it immediately into the stool, pulled the flush chain, and together we stood quietly aside, four hands cupped to four wide-open ears.

When the report came I swear we were taken aback in utter unison, both flinching as if a pair of subterranean hands had slapped our faces simultaneously. The explosion, though muffled, carried with it something that suggested potency; Carter recognized this, and so did I. Grinning, we shook hands.

Because he had not posed a second question — What damage, if any, might exploding the secret weapon inflict? — Carter's grin turned to surprise when we noticed that the small room was filling rapidly with water.

Time to leave, Carter said, and we left, not bothering to switch off any of the lights. At the back door I paused and looked back. Water was spreading from the small bathroom into the large square concrete basement, looking for the lowest depression to fill it, to make it equal, you know, as water will.

With morning comes birdsong and sunshine and the sound of something more than a trickle in the current just off the shore. We open our eyes, all four of us, at pretty much the same time. Our Captain sits up in his sleeping bag, rubs his eyes, yawns. Though we had not spent a lot of time on the water in the sunshine yesterday, already our Captain's round fair face has begun to burn.

We had a storm last night, I tell the Skipper. Wind and rain. Lightning struck a cottonwood.

With reddened eyes our Captain surveys the inside of the tent — brown canvas sagging, water in several small ponds on the floor, duffel bags having been clawed at leaning at precarious angles against each other — then nods, as much as to say he believes me.

Then that explains the frogs, our Captain says.

The frogs? This in chorus from the yeomen.

Yes, our Captain says. He pauses to scratch. He is wearing what he wore yesterday in the boat—blue bib overalls and red tennis shoes. He is keeping us in suspense, but not deliberately; our Captain can do but one thing at a time, and at the moment he is digging at something, both hands lost but ferociously at work behind the bib of the overalls.

Frogs, he says at last, withdrawing the hands. For a minute he examines his nails, as if he expects to discover something lying dormant beneath them, something heretofore unknown to science, something alive and just now emerging. Last night, he continues, speaking to the nails, there were frogs in my sleeping bag. One by one I caught them and threw them out the door and into the river.

You were dreaming, says the owner of the sagging tent.

You were drunk, says my brother.

You were neither, I say. You were our Captain, doing what you had to do to preserve us from a deadly if not Biblical Great Frog Infestation.

Our Captain smiles broadly. Bullshit, he says, and with that the day officially begins.

Sunshine. Windless. The words are magic. Sun + shine = sun shining. Simple addition, I believe. Wind + less = no wind.

Under sunshine on a windless morning four pioneer spirits move and have their being in unplanned harmony. My brother with his keen eye locates firewood dry enough to burn, his efforts encouraged by a can of starter fluid intended for the charcoal we neglected to bring. Leon with his own keen eye finds skillet and utensils, eggs and bacon and the essentials for flapjacks—and the coffee pot. The Skipper goes down

130

to his ship and with a two-pound Folgers can begins the bailing. I strike the tent and spread it out beyond the cottonwoods, in the sunshine, where each of us in turn will lay those personal belongings dampened if not drenched by the storm.

I am examining the felled cottonwood when Leon and my brother sound a clarion call for breakfast. The lightning had struck the tree about twenty feet from the ground, a direct hit (I imagine God putting his eye on a Norden bombsight and, having given Himself the thumbs up—Bombs away!— squeezing the button), and the sprawling upper two-thirds of that noble indigenous creature had come creaking and groaning downward, crashing its multitudinous twigs and limbs into the shoreline's dark fertile topsoil, one of the larger branches striking not more than a dozen paces from where we had pitched the tent.

Breakfast lifts our high spirits higher. Black coffee hot enough to scorch the lips. Bacon only slightly burned. Eggs over—this way and that. And flapjacks, their staple ingredients brought together with a milk substitute—Lone Star beer.

If our Captain had ever experienced a single moment of surliness in his entire three decades of fruition and decadence you would not know it now. He eats several of everything, then politely requests another round. And why shouldn't he be the wide-angled picture of felicitude? He has had a good night's sleep. The sun is shining. The gear, beneath the sun, lies drying. The *Diamond* has been bailed and swabbed. The food apparently is much to his liking. And the river is rising.

Though the river is flowing not more than twenty feet from where we sit at the fire, savoring breakfast, the Skipper, who has spent upwards of fifteen minutes in the *Diamond* bailing, gives us a complete report.

The river is rising, he tells us, probably, he says, because of last night's rain. At the moment, he says, the *Diamond-in-the-Rough* sits moored in a channel plenty deep enough to float her.

We yeomen nod at this news, and smile. The Skipper smiles, too, revealing flapjack.

Behind every dark cloud, says the Skipper, apparently unable to resist at least one platitude, lies a silver lining.

We yeomen nod—and smile. And the only free cheese, my brother says, apparently unable to stifle the non sequitur, is in the mousetrap.

When the coffee pot runs dry we check the gear to note that it, too, is sufficiently dry, so like a well-oiled machine we break camp and begin to load the boat. Not more than an hour or so later Leon unties the line from its mooring—an exposed root belonging, no doubt, to one of the cotton-woods, maybe that one struck down by lightning—and with a shout embodying relief and expectation we are off.

The Skipper had sounded the channel correctly; it carries us a few feet away from the shore, then bends slowly to port, then straightens to begin a stretch that looks to go on forever. If you are a beachcomber out for a late-morning stroll, and you have both a camera and a desire to record this moment, and if the film is not outdated, the finished product might look something like this: a silver boat, as long and as wide and as deep as God's mercy, riding moderately high on the crest of a Loup River channel; the owner of the tent and its stakes astride the bow, legs dangling, beard and wide-brimmed straw hat giving him the distinct appearance of a figurehead chiseled skillfully from a trunk of hickory; the boat's Captain, sitting straight-backed and wide-beamed near the center of his craft, his fleshy hands on the oars, his face half-grinning into the sun, absorbing her rays; two brothers occupying the fantail portion of the vessel, one leaning against the chest that contains the beverage, the other, the one with the sailor's cap low on his forehead, pointing to something wedged between the chest and the hull.

No, the beachcomber will tell his children when they ask what it is the man in the funny cap is pointing to. He has no idea.

But the man in the funny cap knows, and so does his brother: it is the packet of detailed relief maps given to the Captain by the State Historical Society, and while yesterday the packet was roughly the size of a Sears catalog, today it has assumed the dimensions of a body long drowned and now woefully bloated.

The channel of course will not last forever, though it will last long enough for the keen edge of our Captain's alertness to become blunted. He releases the oars to lean back against a duffel bag; settled in, he closes his eyes.

One by one we crewmen do pretty much the same. With a sigh the man who owns the tent relinquishes himself as ornament and crawls back to claim a duffel bag of his own. My brother and I half sit, half sprawl, our backs against the chest we had recently opened to treat each other to a post-breakfast beer. With my eyes closed I can sense more than observe our movement, and though the movement is slow and easy and ever so gradually circular I cannot fully relax; against the drum lying deep in the ear I anticipate the sudden flim-flam of Loup River sand scouring the *Diamond*'s keel.

But there is no such foreboding sound, meaning that we are floating, meaning that if we are floating we are neither pulling nor pushing.

My brother's voice is the first to cut into the silence.

Leon, he says, and he waits then until Leon grunts, whereupon my brother continues: Leon, how can you remember to bring the tent but forget the tent stakes? Leon, he says, how is this possible?

Silence.

Leon, my brother says, don't you store the tent stakes with the tent?

Silence.

Leon, my brother says, I know how you can avoid forgetting the tent stakes again. *Wrap them into your tent.*

My brother waits—all of us, with the probable exception of Leon—waits for a response. The *Diamond* meanwhile seems to be reading the channel on her own. With my eyes closed I feel the easy motion of the boat moving not only me, but everything above me, especially the sun. I long to be dizzy, to be darkly and warmly disoriented—forever. Even so, in the interest of avoiding anarchy, I hold fast to the cool steady pillar that is my can of beer.

When Leon finally responds, he asks this question: How many extra tent stakes do we now have?

Brother: Four.

Leon: Why do we have these extra stakes?

Brother: Because we bought them at the hardware store in Central City.

Leon: Why did we buy them at the hardware store in Central City?

Brother: Because you remembered that you forgot the originals.

Leon: And why did I remember?

To this question my brother apparently has no answer. After the boat has described a full half-circle Leon repeats the question. When the circle is completed Leon provides the answer.

Because, he says, I forgot them.

Do all things at last aspire to roundness? I take a long draw on the cold beer, which isn't cold anymore. I have opened my eyes. The universe begins slowly to come into focus— Leon only half visible behind a mound of duffel bag; our Captain half dozing, his shirtless torso, that portion not covered by the bib on the blue overalls, trying in terms of pinkness to equal the pinkness on our Captain's face; my brother under his white cap holding his beer in both hands between his knees, studying the can as if deciphering Truth from an ancient primer. I look then to the near shore, then to the far; on bottomland rich with alluvial soil cattle of many persuasions are grazing—Angus, Hereford, Charolais. This was the valley of the Skidi, the Wolf People, the Pani Loups, and we are floating their river, their Plenty Potatoes River, edible tubers in those days growing wild and abundantly along both shores. Now, crops of corn and milo and soybeans enrich both the earth and the farmer who takes them from it—the farmer who often irrigates his land with water down from the land of the rancher, down from the

Sandhills, where often the rancher must bite his lower lip to permit the installing of a center pivot for the several yearly cuttings of hay necessary to the feeding of the cattle whose meat and milk . . .

If I am not mistaken, the *Diamond* has righted herself and is now floating bow-first downstream. Fully awake, both the near and the far now in focus, I rise slowly to read the channel. I read it with these words:

O my God!

Intensity and inflection: surely in our language these count for as much as mere volume. My fellow Loupers apparently respond to all three — in the blink of an eye they are sitting perfectly upright, their heads as if vanes responding to a sudden change in weather. Our Captain echoes my earlier observation. *O my God!* he says. *The locks!*

Ahead of me I see the locks, a series of guillotines side by side, spanning the river, each lock with a blade as a door that can be raised or lowered to permit or to deny the letting-in of water. Two of the doors are open; I can see their blades suspended a foot or so above the river. So this is why the floating has been so leisurely! Most of the Loup's channels have been dredged and catechized, their several flows thus directed into the mouths of those ominous locks, the single flow beyond the locks becoming a canal from which farmers for a considerable stretch can draw water for irrigation.

Most of this I'll learn pending our survival. For the moment, for several moments, I am busy shouting instructions to our Captain: Hard on the left oar! Hard on the right! Both oars now — straight ahead!

The *Diamond* responds to our Captain's efforts; she begins

to move cross-current toward a jetty of sand not far down-river where the water is parting, its larger portion flowing to the port side of the jetty, the smaller portion to the starboard.

Though the Skipper keeps the bow of the boat at a steady forty-five-degree angle against the current—Heavy on the right oar!—the current moves us downstream as rapidly as the oars propel us toward the jetty. If we can reach the jetty, where surely the water is not as deep as it is further out in the channel, we can probably jump ashore and restrain the *Diamond* before she can be pulled back into the channel and down then to be sucked under one of the lock doors to whatever watery fate might lie beyond. Better yet, if we can reach the smaller stream before we come abreast of the jetty we can continue to float that stream—the Loup that we had heretofore been floating—until we reach our scheduled debarkation point, the Genoa bridge.

The channel is deep and flows swiftly; I can see that the water gains momentum as it nears the locks. I can see also white water thrashing at the mouths of the two locks whose doors are suspended open, and I can hear a steady roaring as the water crashes through the openings.

Our Captain is all business. What he lacks in precision he makes up for in brute strength and determination. Leon does his part meanwhile by lying low; stretched out on his belly, his head at the top of the bow and somewhat raised, he has become now a low-profile figurehead, a hood ornament, so to speak, offering very little resistance to the onrushing breeze. My brother has not moved much; he sits crushing and uncrushing his beer can. I continue to shout instructions to the Skipper, who continues to work the oars as if suddenly he had been dropped into a phalanx of snakes and has thirty seconds, by the watch, to kill them.

Just as we appear to have gained the advantage, the current for some reason quickens, and we are driven sideways further than ever, it seems, from the jetty of sand. Our Captain, however, does not relent. He is unstoppable—a heavy-bodied bird with an inveterate belief that its meager wings might lift it somehow into flight.

If I were not so preoccupied with survival I would be reminded of my father that day he was told he must build for the family an indoor bathroom. He couldn't do it, of course, yet he must do it, and he would. I could see the whole of it that day in his eyes—anger and doubt bookended by spite and resolution.

We make it, our fantail missing the tip of the jetty, according to my brother, who is in the best position to take a measurement, by a full eight inches.

And of the new porcelain bowl
So beautiful
It might have been Christ feeding the multitude.

For some time we do not respond to the sound of sand against the *Diamond*'s keel. Our Captain, winded, rests on his oars; we yeomen sit in a stony and grateful silence. From beyond the sandbar that separates the shallow from the deep I can hear the steady muted roaring of water plunging through the two raised doors of the locks.

It's true: you don't miss the water until the well runs dry.

If yesterday's pulling and pushing of the *Diamond* had

been a challenge, today's is an utter and ongoing consterna-
tion. Most of the Loup's water had been diverted at the locks,
leaving us little more than a trickle in which to navigate our
lovely boat, our leviathan.

There simply is no surcease from the struggle. We pull. We
push. We cajole. We strain. We exhort. We take a break. Our
Captain, much of his body red now where it once was pink,
swears. Well, says Leon, it could be worse; at least we have
cold beer.

Leon, for all his tent stakes, is wrong on one count and only
half correct on the other. The beer is not cold; it is not even
chilly. We had brought along cubes instead of a block, a tactical error that eventually produces strategic consequences. On
the other count Leon is momentarily accurate: we do indeed
have beer. What he fails to append is the following: But under
these conditions we will not have it very long.

Simple arithmetic: sun + shine = sunshine. Boat + absence
of water = physical exhaustion.

We read the channel expertly, as if each of us had been destined from birth to read channels. But not even an aficionado
can carve a true matador from a banana — nor can a reader
of channels witch forth water where there is none. And so it
is that we attempt to float the *Diamond* in a current deep
enough only for dreaming. And so it is that our beer breaks
become increasingly frequent.

Which is why the beer, our last and only consolation, does
not last very long. Which is why the beachcomber with the
camera will have a distinctly different picture to show pos-
terity: my brother and I at the stern, our bodies bent, now
lifting, now shoving; Leon with an oar at the bow, prying,

shoveling; and our Captain within a noose at the end of a rope, bending himself forward as if one of my grandfather's workhorses, straining, straining.

Man was made not only to mourn, but to persist—and, at times, to persist blindly and stubbornly and irrationally. Thus do we push and tug and dig and haul until one of us—our Captain, as it so happens—falls face-down into the damp sand that is the channel and whispers, when finally we manage to turn him over, *Bullshit. I'm done for.*

Snap this one, beachcomber, and make it a close-up: our Captain sitting like a punch-drunk boxer in the sand, sucking air, his faithful yeomen on their knees beside him, each in turn confessing that he too has had quite enough.

When we are minimally revived we pissant the *Diamond* to the closer shore. Underfoot, a thick expanse of acreage speaks to us in the language of grass. I understand. I obey. Why is it that just before I drift into sleep I think of Psalms 23? *He maketh me to lie down in green pastures; he leadeth me beside the still waters.* I wanted to stay awake long enough to make something of this. I wanted to put one and one together to see what improbable sum might occur. Groundwater flowing from Cherry County in the Sandhills had gathered and risen to form one branch of the Loup River, to serpentine its innumerable bends near Brewster and Taylor and Burwell and Ord, to join its sister, the middle branch, below St. Paul, that branch already bolstered by its brother, the south contingent, all three then moving beneath the bridge at Palmer to the bridge at Fullerton, beyond that bridge then to have its bulk diverted to the locks, leaving that trickle we so gallantly and foolishly labored to float the

Diamond in. How old is this bur oak, Granddad—and where did it come from? *Who in this bowling alley bowled the sun?*

But I am exhausted. Lying in the green pasture, beside the still—as in silent—waters, I sleep.

7

The commonplace is the thing, but it's hard to find. — Andrew Wyeth, *The Helga Pictures*

I have floated the Loup River each summer now for almost thirty years — in spite of that near disaster at the locks, in spite of occasional channels with little more than wet sand to buoy the johnboat. At times, when the day is sultry and hot, when even the deepest current seems becalmed, ticks and mosquitoes hold revival meetings along the shores of the Loup, especially in areas of thick vegetation, and frequently the turnouts are spectacular. Often I have drifted thrillingly close to such a gathering, have watched the worshippers roil and swarm, have heard the portentous buzz and hum and babel of their singing and their glossalalia. *There is a fountain filled with blood,* they sing (I have heard them), and the blood they speak of is in the vein and the artery of the Louper passing by. *Throw out the lifeline,* they sing (I have heard them), but they have no intention of rescuing the sinner; they want only to haul him in to shore to devour him.

The trick here is to avoid joining the congregation, to float instead to a bank relatively free of brush and undergrowth, to an expansive pallet of bunchgrass or ryegrass, say, cast half in shadow by a few towering grandmother cottonwoods. Pitch the tents. Distribute and organize the gear. Gather firewood. Build a fire. Bathe in the river. Pop open a beer.

143

The one with the Martin guitar picks at each string, tuning and tightening, then strums and loosens and tightens until his toothy grin says: I am satisfied. Another slips a harmonica from his hip pocket, taps it against his palm, fits it into his mouth as if to taste the first full fruit of a season's abundance. And where is the banjo? Over there, in the hands of the kid too young to play the banjo. But he does, firelight flickering against the banjo's silver head like a friendly semaphore.

"Sandhills Rag." "Nebraska Skies." "Sweet Mother Earth." And

Get back to the well,
Every now and then—
When your spirit is dry
And your mind is growing dim . . .

One summer the well at flood stage damn near took all of us under, for good. After the experience at the locks we learned to begin the float further upstream—under the Palmer Bridge, at the park near St. Paul, or a couple of times all the way up-river near Cotesfield or Scotia. The routes have varied, and so too the makeup of the voyagers—and the dangers, also, and the pleasures. At certain times it is difficult to know where the danger ends and the pleasure begins.

One summer we stood on a high bank under tarps to watch hail the size of hen eggs transform the river into a low wide-angled calliope. We had delayed mooring the boats (we were a force of six that summer, two canoes and my 12-foot johnboat, christened *Our Lady of the Loup*, and the month was May, because after the experience at the locks we learned to begin to float earlier, when the chances for good upstream water are better), and the price we paid was a thorough soaking; so we stood under the tarps, shivering, watching the hailstones puncture unmercifully the skin of a body of water all morning we had drifted on, watching in awe the body as if its own grandiose physician heal itself, until the storm at last shrugged its thick billowing shoulders and lumbered off to the east-southeast, leaving us to collect our wits around the spit and the whittle of a long evening's campfire.

"Blackberry Blossom." "Autumn Leaves." "Red-Haired Boy." "Devil's Dream."

One night one summer I lay awake well after the campfire's final coal expired thinking of why one of us had remained at home: his first child had been born with most of its organs misplaced, and during the few days that the infant lived only one attempt short of potent medication had served to calm him—the playing of a simple tape of birdsong. I went to sleep thinking of the child yielding to sleep at the melodies of birdsong, and I awoke to birdsong—and quietly I arose and pushed back the tent flaps and on bare feet walked to the edge of the river to watch the sun burn through a layer of fog to reveal the branch where perhaps the bird had perched to do its singing. At the infant's funeral I had stood stunned at the size of the white downy casket, at its no-size, at its bird-sized content, the combination of nest and fledgling too inconsiderable not to be shocked by, marveled at, wept over.

The Loup angler checks his line, checks it again, returns with two catfish sleek as love, in a single motion of pliers and filet knife cleans them, in another motion has them in foil sizzling on the fire.

And you begin to think
It's time your time has come—
Get back to the well
From where your spirit has come . . .

Here is the first of two questions: What lake or pond might fairly be the still-water equivalent of the running-water Loup?

Here is the first of two answers: Maggie's Pond.

I have fished and splashed and contemplated the inconsistencies of the universe at many lakes and ponds, foremost among them Lake Leba and Lake Thomas, both in Nebraska. At these I have hiked and bird-watched, have tracked relentlessly the curlew and the cottontail and the walking stick, have watched my children crawl like box turtles from the lakes' white beaches into their clear shallows, from the shallows dog-paddle then swim sure-finned as minnows into the depths. But Maggie's Pond, in south-central Kansas north and west of my hometown, is finally my choice.

The pond is not really one pond, but three, each of them not much larger than a tire patch, each spring fed, each within an easy stone's throw of one another. They lie in a valley on farmland owned and worked by my wife's aunt's son and his wife; but Aunt Maggie it was who dredged the ponds and who fished them with a patience and a passion akin to religion, and who with her sisters would not leave the table until the bones of the day's catch lay on the plates like an artist's rendition of prototypical skeletons. At the ponds on a calm evening my sons and their wives and my daughters and their husbands, and their children with them, pitch their tents, tents that bloom suddenly like blowout penstemon on the Nebraska

Sandhills, and they loll and they fish and they talk, under a full family moon their voices carrying all the way to the edge of creation. And they sing, too: *Bullfrog, bunchgrass, catfish, carp—play it on your banjo, play it on your harp.* Earlier, one of the boys had caught a four-pound bass on a surface lure, a jitterbug, his infant daughter above and behind him in a backpack beaming as if she deserved the credit. Later, after the laughter in the tents has settled itself into sleep, someone will roll over and wake up and think to check the set lines: *There's a beacon in my bobber, let it shine, let it shine; there's a beacon in my bobber, let it shine.* Jesus, one of the children will say, the sun up, evidence of sleep yet at the corners of the child's eyes, Jesus! That must be the biggest catfish in all the world!

One summer my brother and I, dozing, rammed broadside into an enormous cottonwood snag, capsizing *Our Lady* so quickly and so completely that neither of us could rescue the beer. We had capsized before, certainly, but never quite like this—never so totally unaware, never so suddenly or so thoroughly, and never in a current so swift or in water so deep. We did what the knowledgeable seaman does: we clung to the johnboat as if our lives depended on it, which maybe they did. Most of the gear remained tied down under the boat, but some of it—including the chest of beverage—found individual channels and bobbed away. We stayed with *Our Lady*, white water on either side, until the channel, sensing a bar, began a slow starboard crossing, whereupon my brother and I declined, permitting ourselves to be eased against the sand. Well, I said, that was a helluva trip, wasn't it? My brother allowed that it was—though it did not compare, he said, to that extended tour he took one afternoon in a Hudson Terraplane at the bottom of Ely's Sandpit. Lord! He remembered.

"Steam-Powered Aeroplane." "Okie Boy." "Peaceful Easy Feeling."

Here is the second of two questions: When a small channel breaks from the river, and goes off on its own, and you cannot see where it is going or how far, should you take it?

Here is the second of two answers: No.

One summer we therefore took it, and so immaculate was the journey that we named the overall adventure The Year of the Idyll. The narrow channel with its well-defined banks took us through a meadowland cut from the pages of a child's picture book—assuming that the book is in technicolor, and that its clean clear water moves slowly as if a fatted snake, and that the movement lasts the better part of a lifetime. Tiny flowers that none of us could identify, together with grasses and ground covers equally elusive, crowded this fertile bottom land to the point of bursting. And there seemed to be no end. I think I remember my brother removing the watch from his wrist and tossing it overboard, pronouncing an end to Time. I think I remember that by way of agreeing the rest of us did the same.

An hour before what might have been midnight one of the crew brings forth a bottle of homemade chokecherry wine. The Louper with the harmonica blows spit from the instrument, taps it against his palm, slips it into his hip pocket. Now he is ready with the rest of us to receive the wine. The winemaker is generous, pouring a large amount into each cup, assuring us as he moves around the circle that he has plenty more.

We sip on the wine and talk. The campfire, now a deep bed of white-hot coals, had been a *good* fire, certainly, perhaps even a *great* fire. Where is the line between the good and the great? Who draws it? If a camper is in the woods, and the night is cold, and he builds a fire, is the heat from the fire ever enough to keep him warm if he is alone? The stars are out tonight, thick almost as the tiny flowers that dotted the meadow we floated through that Year of the Idyll. My brother challenges his buddy from Colorado: Five bucks say I can name all seven of the dwarfs in under sixty seconds. My brother's buddy sits on a wooden stool he assembled to perfection with his own hands. Behind his red beard his brain verily whirrs. Well, he says finally, when the whirring stops, he reckons he'll just have to take that bet, and my brother begins his recitation—begins it slowly, as if a litany, as if he had been catechized by Father Lightbody himself. (My brother did not wed the lovely Catholic woman from Denver. He lost his heart, and all other vitals appended thereto, to another.) *Bashful.* Leon the Time-keeper keeps time by counting aloud: 14, 15, 16, 17. *Dopey. Doc.* My brother hesitates waveringly between each name. 28, 29, 30. *Grumpy.* My brother's buddy from Colorado scratches his beard; perhaps he is growing concerned. All of us happen to know that he is down to his last five dollars. 47, 48, 49. *Sneezy.* My brother grimaces. He closes his eyes, as if in the darkness he might better see the final two dwarfs. 52, 53, 54. *Sleepy.* My brother grimaces again, this time attaching a soft low groan to the grimace, a groan that he sustains with an alarming authenticity, especially when one knows that the bet has been rigged, that my brother's brother had planted the seed and nurtured it with a written list of the dwarfs' names, a list that my brother had committed to memory in a flash. 57, 58. My brother increases the intensity of the groan and the breadth of the grimace; in his white cap he looks like a sailor trying desperately to pass not only the seed but the entire peach. An instant before the timekeeper says *60!* my brother shouts *Happy!* and reaches forth his right hand, palm up, to collect his winnings.

In the morning I will awaken to the sound of rain against the tent top. For an hour or more I will lie in my sleeping bag, listening to the rain, drifting into and out of sleep. But the morning is yet to happen. What matters, just now, is the moment, and the moment is ripe with silences heightened by song.

When I need to walk
I can walk with the river,
And when I need to talk
I can talk to the river . . .

My touchstone for the measuring of all small rivers was that stretch of current my fellow Loupers and I dreamed and swirled on almost thirty years ago, before we looked up to see a hydra-headed guillotine grinning its two lost teeth before us. I sort through the beachcomber's pictures to find the correct one, the moment of more than truth, the epiphany. Here it is: a silver boat as long as she is wide and as deep as God's mercy, riding moderately high on the crest of a Loup River channel; the owner of the tent and its stakes astride the bow, legs dangling, beard and wide-brimmed straw hat giving him the distinct appearance of a figurehead chiseled skillfully from a trunk of hickory; the boat's Captain, sitting straight-backed and wide-beamed near the center of his craft, his fleshy hands on the oars, his face half-grinning into the sun, absorbing her rays; two brothers occupying the fantail portion of the vessel, one leaning against the chest that contains the beverage, the other, the one with a sailor's cap low on his forehead, pointing to something wedged between the chest and the hull. What the picture cannot reveal: the easy motion of the boat moving not only me, but everything above me, especially the sun. I longed at that instant to be dizzy, to be darkly and warmly disoriented—forever. And it is that instant that overwhelms all others, including the night's savage wind, the crack and the fall of the cottonwood, the guillotine grinning its two lost teeth before us.

> *When I need a home*
> *I can live with the river,*
> *And when I need to sleep*
> *I can dream by the river.*
>   *Drifting away—*
> *Mother Nature delivers . . .*

That's my older son singing his own song, a cappella, his harmonica asleep in its hip pocket. All the others are asleep, too, I believe, except for me and the singer and the singer's brother, who has retired his banjo in favor of poking the waning coals with a length of barkless cottonwood rescued at midafternoon from the river. Under a full Loup moon, and above the faint glow from the coals, the white wood shines like the body of something almost human.

We fathom you not — we love you — there is perfection in you also,
You furnish your parts toward eternity,
Great or small, you furnish your parts toward the soul.
—Walt Whitman, "Crossing Brooklyn Ferry"

Recently — to celebrate a special anniversary — my wife and I indulged ourselves with a Caribbean cruise. Our enormous liner exuded more glitz and dissipation than Father Lightbody might fairly be expected to expiate in a month of Sundays. We sunbathed and we shopped and we rubbernecked our fellow adventurers until fathom by fathom our corporeal vessels overflowed. Strobe and twang, belly and bikini and gratuity and the lift and the fall, the lilt and the sway of the ship, the creak and the groan and the shivering of more than timbers. At times I felt returned to the waters of the womb, at other times freshly relieved of it — out of its cradle, Walt Whitman, endlessly rocking.

The cruise was fun. The brochures bright almost as my grandmother's seed catalogs said the voyage would be, and it was: in the exercise room, hope in one hand and a rum swizzler in the other, I walked a treadmill — body moving, going nowhere; at regular intervals the Captain from the bridge asked for our attention in a Latino voice so stentorian, and over an intercom so devoted to volume, we had no choice but to cover our ears and listen. Latitude and longitude and rectitude. Twenty knots in the general direction of Eden. And beneath the keel, more than one thousand feet directly down, the floor of the Caribbean.

If there is magic on this planet, it is contained in water. Each evening as the sun neared the horizon my wife and I studied the blueness of the Caribbean, took notes on it in silence without pad or pencil, filing the notes away somewhere in the handiest cortex of the brain. If her sense of water runs as deep as mine, I pity the poor bastard boatswain whose paycheck will be deferred until he sounds it.

One of those evenings, recording notes without taking them, I remembered a news account I had run across a year or so ago. It appeared under the general heading of Human Interest, and it told of a Baptist preacher somewhere in the Deep South who in the process of baptizing his sparse congregation at the edge of a river held one of them under a bit too long; when the frightened sinner floundered, the preacher released him and he drifted away screaming and soon located the principal current and drowned. A compelling combination of the mortal and the immortal, I thought, flesh shouting its reluctance into the cool quotient of the spirit. And I wondered if the baptism had been sufficiently and well enough performed for it to have taken hold and thus last, like a childhood vaccination. Trinity: code name for the testing of the atomic bomb in New Mexico. In the name of the Father, and of the Son, and . . .

And I wondered too about my own Father—dead since 9 December 1990, his brown Dodge broadsided by a drunk—who with two fingers missing on his right hand had grappled me out of Simpson's Pond in south-central Kansas to arrange me on a pallet of bunchgrass to pump water from me as if from a cistern: to what extent might he have sacrificed a part of himself for me?

God knows I don't know. I know only that at sunset the Caribbean, though somewhat vaster and deeper and bluer than Simpson's Pond, should not permit itself to become uppity: it can only become larger than the sum of its parts when those parts come together. Above it meanwhile the Rockies in Colorado and in Wyoming's Snowy Range are contributing their parts drop by eternal drop to the ultimate cistern, to the myriad touchstones of wetness, these to be joined by the Sandhill waters of the North and Middle Loups in Nebraska, all then (but not all finally) snaking and braiding their way to become John Neihardt's Missouri, John yielding himself willingly to become Mark Twain's Mississippi, Mississippi then losing itself to the Caribbean, and that to the greater Atlantic, loss in its own inscrutable way thus returning a profit, a dividend, while my kinfolk, those creatures of the deep both bone and otherwise that I cannot see but know are there, swim on, swim on.